Spirit & Dream Animals

© JASON FELL

About Richard Webster

Author of over forty titles published with Llewellyn, Richard Webster is one of New Zealand's most prolific writers. His best-selling books include *Spirit Guides & Angel Guardians*, *Creative Visualization for Beginners*, *Soul Mates*, *Is Your Pet Psychic?*, *Practical Guide to Past-Life Memories*, *Astral Travel for Beginners*, *Miracles*, and the four-book series on archangels: *Michael*, *Gabriel*, *Raphael*, and *Uriel*.

A noted psychic, Richard is a member of the National Guild of Hypnotherapists (USA), the Association of Professional Hypnotherapists and Parapsychologists (UK), the International Registry of Professional Hypnotherapists (Canada), and the Psychotherapy and Hypnotherapy Institute of New Zealand. When not touring, he resides in New Zealand with his wife and family.

Richard Webster

Spirit & Dream Animals

DECIPHER THEIR MESSAGES, DISCOVER YOUR TOTEM

Llewellyn Publications
Woodbury, Minnesota

FIRST EDITION
First Printing, 2011

Cover art © Colin Mayne Illustration
Cover design by Lisa Novak

Llewellyn Publications is a registered trademark of Llewellyn Worldwide Ltd.

Library of Congress Cataloging-in-Publication Data

Webster, Richard, 1946–
 Spirit & dream animals : decipher their messages, discover your totem / Richard Webster. — 1st ed.
    p.   cm.
 Includes bibliographical references and index.
 ISBN 978-0-7387-2770-7
 1. Animals—Miscellanea. 2. Totems—Miscellanea. 3. Dream interpretation.
 I. Title. II. Title: Spirit and dream animals.
 BF1623.A55W43 2011
 133'.259—dc23
                        2011022292

Llewellyn Worldwide Ltd. does not participate in, endorse, or have any authority or responsibility concerning private business transactions between our authors and the public.
 All mail addressed to the author is forwarded, but the publisher cannot, unless specifically instructed by the author, give out an address or phone number.
 Any Internet references contained in this work are current at publication time, but the publisher cannot guarantee that a specific location will continue to be maintained. Please refer to the publisher's website for links to authors' websites and other sources.

Llewellyn Publications
A Division of Llewellyn Worldwide Ltd.
2143 Wooddale Drive
Woodbury, MN 55125-2989
www.llewellyn.com

Printed in the United States of America

Other books by Richard Webster

For my good friend Jim Hainey

Contents

Introduction

I was walking along Connaught Road in Hong Kong one summer's day about ten years ago. Because it was hot and humid, I went into a café to have a coffee in air-conditioned comfort. As I sipped my drink, I became aware of the couple sitting next to me. An attractive Chinese woman was telling her American friend about animal dreaming. Apparently, if an Asian woman dreamt about an animal shortly before becoming pregnant, the child would exhibit the qualities of that particular animal.[1]

I was intrigued, and after apologizing for overhearing the conversation, I joined in. I had been interested in dreams for many years but had not given any thought to the different animals that appear in our dreams. The two women had gone to college together, and had not seen each other for several years. The American lady was on vacation, and her friend, Lee Tang, was enjoying showing her around Hong Kong. They had been catching up on everything that had happened in their lives since last seeing each other. I happened to overhear their conversation at exactly the right time.

I learned that Chinese dream interpretation is called *zhan meng shu*, and is a small part of *fangshu*, the divinatory arts. It is believed that dreams are caused by a lack of energy. This occurs when one of the five elements of our makeup are out of balance. The colors that appear in the dream indicate the organ that is not working as well as it should be. If the dream is suffused with a red color, for example, the heart will be out of balance. (Green relates to the liver, the spleen to yellow, the lungs to white, and the kidneys to black.)

However, the dreams dreamt by a woman who is about to conceive, or has just conceived, are not caused by a lack of energy. In fact, they create energy. They are prophetic dreams that provide valuable clues about the destiny of the unborn child.

Lee Tang leaned across to me. "Did you know that Buddha's mother dreamt of a gorgeous white elephant with six tusks that ran around her bed three times? That's a classic example of a prophetic animal dream."

"Do all pregnant women have animal dreams?" I asked.

Lee Tang shook her head. "Only if the child shows promise. It is a sign of great potential. However, I think all women have dreams about their unborn babies. It used to be a sign of misfortune if the mother experienced no such dreams." She smiled and held up a finger. "The mother has to keep the dream a secret. My mother hasn't told me about her dreams about me. She's told me she had them, and they were good, but that's all I know."

When I returned to my hotel, I wrote down as much as I could remember of the conversation. I spoke to several people about the subject, but learned no more. Every now and again, over the years, I reread my notes on animal dreaming but added very little to them.

While in Singapore recently, I was introduced to someone who specializes in interpreting *t'aimeng*, predictive dreams about unborn children. Her fascinating stories rekindled my interest, and provided the necessary inspiration to write this book.

An unusual dream was the final motivating factor. Shortly after returning home, I dreamt I was driving my car into the city. The car in front of me on the freeway had a personalized license plate: *ANIMAL*. A week later, I happened to be driving along the same stretch of freeway and noticed that the car in front of me had a different personalized plate: *ANAMAL*. The spelling was different, but it seemed like a good omen. I started this book the very next day.

Although animal dreams are extremely popular in the East, particularly in China, Korea, Taiwan, and Japan, they can be found in all parts of the world and throughout history. The mother of Alexander the Great, for instance, dreamt that she was sleeping with Amun Ra, the horned god.

Men can experience birth dreams also. In a dream, Philip of Macedon saw an imperial seal surrounding a lion on his wife's womb shortly before his son, destined to become Alexander the Great, was born.

A man also dreamt what is probably the most famous birth dream of all. This is the dream that Joseph experienced after learning that Mary, his wife, was pregnant: "The angel of the Lord appeared unto him in a dream, saying, Joseph, thou son of David, fear not to take unto thee Mary thy wife: for that which is conceived in her is of the Holy Ghost. And she shall bring forth a son, and thou shalt call his name JESUS: for he shall save his people from their sins" (Matthew 1:20–21).

People have been fascinated by dreams for thousands of years. In every part of the world, people believed their dreams must have meaning. As in most other ancient civilizations, the Chinese believed that dreams could predict future events. The emperor employed interpreters to help him understand the meanings of his dreams. Three thousand years ago, an unknown poet wrote the *Shi Jing*, or *Book of Poems*, which contained a great deal of information about dreams, especially animal dreams. He recorded that dreaming of a bear was a sign that the child would be a boy. Dreaming of a snake signified the birth of a girl. Both were considered equally good omens.

In the East, scientific analysis of dreams began during the Warring States Period (475 BCE–221 BCE). Xun Zi, a famous philosopher, wrote his book *Jie Bi* at this time. In it he said that dreams were mental activities created by the mind, while it was in a relaxed, peaceful state. Up until that time it was thought that dreams always predicted future events.

Wang Fu, a dream interpreter during the Eastern Han dynasty, wrote a book called *Qian Fu Lun* (On Human Potentials), in which he described ten different types of dreams. Although he was not the first person to classify dreams, his system was the most comprehensive and is still being used today. Wang Fu believed that every dream contained a message that could be interpreted.

Wang Fu's Classification System

1. *Direct dreams.* Someone dreams of something that later occurs in his or her life.

2. *Symbolic dreams.* The symbols in these dreams need to be interpreted. For instance, dreaming of fish symbolizes abundance, while dreaming of rats symbolizes negative influences.

3. *Focused dreams.* If someone thinks extensively about something, he or she is likely to experience dreams about the topic. Consequently, it is better to think positive thoughts, rather than negative ones, to ensure that your dreams are happy ones.

4. *Dreams of intention.* If someone is working hard at a project, he or she is likely to continue working on it in his or her dreams. A salesperson working hard to make an important sale, for instance, is likely to experience dreams about it.

5. *Status dreams.* Wang Fu felt that the meanings of dreams varied because of the position held in society by the dreamer. An academic would benefit by dreaming of a dragon, as it portends upward progress. However, a dragon is powerful. Consequently, it could be negative for a lowly peasant to dream of a dragon, as he might be harmed by someone in a position of power.

6. *Climatic dreams.* Wang Fu believed that external stimuli could affect our dreams. Someone who falls asleep on a cold night with the wind raging outside could expect to experience gloomy dreams.

7. *Seasonal dreams.* People can expect to have dreams related to the seasons. In springtime, people are likely to dream of beautiful, lush landscapes and happy outdoor activities. In winter, they are more likely to dream of sitting around a fire to keep warm.

8. *Sickness dreams.* When people are ill, they are likely to experience unpleasant dreams involving strange animals and disasters of various sorts.

9. *Opposite dreams.* People sometimes experience dreams that are completely opposite to the real situation. A young man might dream of losing his lover, when in fact the relationship is becoming closer all the time.

10. *Personality dreams.* People are likely to experience dreams that accord with their nature. A kindly person will dream of performing good deeds, while a criminal might dream of stealing from others.

When Buddhism reached China, it brought with it a large amount of material on dreams. This included the Buddhist belief that life itself was a dream. Ideas like this were extraordinary to the pragmatic, down-to-earth Chinese. It was easier for them to accept the Buddha's explanation that dreams are connected to what we eat, and can be affected by our sleeping posture. Taoism also contained a large amount of information on dreams, and dream books were written by Taoists that were intended to undermine the precepts of Buddhism. These books claimed, for instance, that it was a bad portent to dream of a Buddhist monk.[2]

Predictions of Dreams was written at this time. Zhou Xuan's book made him famous because it was the first to describe the meanings of dream symbols. Although his book contained only fifty symbols, it marked the start of a huge industry of books on dream interpretations.

In the West and Middle East, interest in dreams was just as high. Four-thousand-year-old papyri, now in the British Museum, contain dream interpretations that demonstrate the ancient Egyptian belief that dreams predicted the future. Archaeologists found a dream guide in the library of King Ashurbanipal (seventh century BCE) in the ruins of the city of Nineveh.[3]

The *Epic of Gilgamesh*, dating back to the first millennium BCE, tells the story of Gilgamesh, the most famous of all Mesopotamian heroes. It contains numerous accounts of different dreams, many containing divine messages concerning danger and potential victories.

According to the Bible, Joseph correctly interpreted the Pharaoh's dreams that foretold seven plentiful and seven lean years (Genesis 41:17–38). The prophet Daniel also gave a correct interpretation of King Nebuchadnezzar's dreams as a prediction that the king's pride would contribute to his seven years of madness (Daniel 4:5–35).

Some biblical dreams were revelations from God. When Jacob dreamt about angels ascending and descending a ladder that went all the way to heaven, God appeared and told him that he and his descendants would be given the land where he lay sleeping (Genesis 28:12–16). The Book of Job tells how God could speak directly to individuals during their dreams: "In a dream, in a vision of the night, when deep sleep falleth upon men, in slumberings upon the bed; then he openeth the ears of men, and sealeth their instruction, that he may withdraw man from his purpose, and hide pride from man" (Job 33:15–17).[4]

Until the end of the Middle Ages, Christians believed that dreams could be divinely inspired. At that time, the Church decided that the revelation of God could come only through the Church.

Christianity was not the only religion that believed dreams held spiritual significance. According to Buddhist legend, Queen Maya knew she had conceived a son when she dreamt that a white elephant had descended into her womb. The son grew up to become Buddha.

Plato (c. 428–347 BCE), the Greek philosopher, believed that the seat of dreams resided in the liver. He believed some dreams came directly from the gods, but others were created by the "lawless wild-beast nature which peers out in sleep."[5]

In the second century CE, Artemidorus, a Greek geographer, wrote five influential books on dream interpretation called *Oneirocritica* (*oneiros* means "dream" in Greek). A Greek cult that believed that dreaming could help cure illnesses became so influential that at least six hundred temples were used for rites and sacrifices to ensure that the right dreams were dreamt to create a cure. The ancient Greeks also regularly consulted oracles to find out the meanings of their dreams.

Of course, even back then, not everyone believed in the divinatory or healing powers of dreams. Aristotle (384–322 BCE), in his book *On Dreams*, anticipated the work of Sigmund Freud by writing that dreams were subject to emotional distortions. The Roman statesman Marcus Tullius Cicero (106–43 BCE) wrote a book called *De Divinatione*, which attacked and ridiculed dream interpretation.

Lucretius (1st century BCE), a Roman philosopher, came to the conclusion that dreams dealt with whatever it was we were interested in during the day, or to satisfy bodily needs.

Over a thousand years later, Moses Maimonides (1135–1204) felt that dreams were the actions of an "imaginary faculty" that came into play while we were asleep.

René Descartes (1596–1650), the French rationalist philosopher, claimed that the body and mind were separate, and that this dualism was an argument for immortality. He is best known for saying, "*Cogito ergo sum*" (I think, therefore I am). Descartes believed that the mind was always active, even during sleep.

A new era of dream research began in 1899, when Sigmund Freud (1856–1939) finished his monumental, 250,000-word work, *The Interpretation of Dreams*. The opening words of this book are: "In the pages that follow I shall bring forward proof that there is a psychological technique which makes it possible to interpret dreams." The book took Freud three years to write, and he considered it one of his best works. In 1931 he wrote, "Insight such as this falls to one's lot but once in a lifetime."

Freud felt that our dreams disguised hidden, latent meanings that were concealed during the day but became visible at night in the form of dreams. These were usually unconscious, infantile wishes.

Carl Jung (1875–1961), Freud's most famous student, disagreed with some aspects of Freud's dream theories. He believed that dreams were natural occurrences that did not necessarily contain hidden meanings. Even when they did, there was no standard meaning for each symbol that appeared, because the interpretations depended on both the dream and the dreamer. Jung also noticed that people frequently dream of helpful animals, or animal-headed people, when they are ill. In some way, these animals symbolize the healing process.

Alfred Adler (1870–1937), who was also at one time a follower of Freud, saw dreams as being a particular type of thought that reflected the dreamer's current situation, goals, and approach to life.

Fritz Perls (1893–1970), the American psychiatrist, was the founder of gestalt therapy. He believed that everything in a person's dreams was a projection of the person's own self. Consequently, dreams are created by the emotions, and any symbolic content in them comes from the person's own daytime experiences.

The association between eye movement and dreams had been known since 1892,[6] but it was not until the 1950s that scientists began studying it seriously. Experiments in sleep laboratories show that mental activity continues throughout the night, but that dreaming occurs during stages of rapid eye movement (REM). People who are woken up while in the REM stage of their sleep remember their dreams about 80 percent of the time.[7] This has enabled researchers to collect enormous quantities of information, but so far they have not been able to explain how or why we all dream. However, dreaming is an essential part of life. People who are deprived of the REM portions of their sleep suffer from anxiety, tiredness, memory loss, and have poor concentration.

The connection between animals and humans is a basic belief of shamanism. The shaman uses his power animal, or guardian spirit, to connect with the animal world to do his work. This frequently happens in dreams. In the dreams of the Cocopa of the Colorado River valley, for instance, animals appear as human beings.[8] The Jívaro people of South America find that a guardian spirit usually appears first as an animal, and then appears as a human being in a dream.[9] The Jívaro believe that if an animal speaks to you, it is conclusive evidence that it is your power animal. It is not surprising that animals can appear in human form in our dreams, as we are both living on this planet together and are related in myriads of different ways.

For the Australian Aborigines, "Dreamtime" was the time when the world was fresh and new, and ancestor spirits created form and shape to the land. Some of these mythic beings were people, while others were totem animals. These ancestor spirits had the ability to change from person to animal, and decide what they wanted to be after experiencing life in both human and animal form.

At a deep level, animals still remember making their choice. The great fertility mothers and male genitors created the first people. These mythic figures are eternal, and even though some are killed, disappear, or change shape in the Aboriginal mythic stories, their integral qualities remain. They are spiritually just as alive today as they ever were, and the places where they metamorphosed became sacred grounds. In the Dreamtime, man is just one part of nature, and is not considered especially different from the mythic people and animals that live there. The land still retains its memories of the Dreamtime, as do the Aboriginal people. Everyone is given an animal spirit at birth, and this provides guidance, wisdom, and protection.

Power animals are always beneficial. They exist to help you in every way they can as you make your path through life. Pay attention to your animal dreams. Be aware of your guardian animals while you are awake as well. Call on them whenever necessary and make them an integral part of your life. Every aspect of your life will be enhanced as a result.

Part One

CHAPTER ONE

The Importance of Dreams

We all dream every night. In fact, we have several lengthy dreams every single night.[1] Some people claim that they never dream, but this is not the case. Dreams quickly fade from our memories. Researchers at the University of Chicago did an experiment with ten volunteers that demonstrates this. Over a period of fifty-one nights, the volunteers were woken up at different times. When they were woken up during periods of REM sleep, they were able to provide detailed descriptions of their dreams on forty-six out of fifty-four occasions. However, when they were awakened five minutes after the REM stage, no detailed accounts were given, although on nine of eleven occasions "fragments" were recalled. Woken up ten or more minutes after the REM stage, only one dream fragment was obtained from twenty-six occasions.[2]

Scientists have also demonstrated that people who are prevented from dreaming, by being woken up every time they enter the REM stage, become unwell. This shows that our dreams are essential for our physical and mental well-being. As a result of this, there is a theory that we go to sleep solely to dream. If true, this shows that our dreams are at least as important to us as the thoughts we think while we are awake.

Our dreams are important to us but usually hold little interest to others. If you have ever seen someone's eyes glaze over while you were telling him or her about your latest dream, you will know what I mean.

The mysterious, almost surreal quality of dreams makes them an endless source of fascination, and it is not surprising that people have been trying to analyze and understand them from prehistoric times.

Daydreams are important also, and play a valuable part in our lives. However, their impact on our lives is not as profound as that of the dreams that occur while we are asleep. When we are sleeping and have temporarily let go of our everyday lives, our dreams allow us to see aspects of ourselves that we either conceal or possibly do not know exist. Our dreams can reveal amazing insights. They help us handle the stresses and pressures of everyday life. They allow us to express our frustrations, fears, and anger in a way that does not hurt others. They can protect us by providing glimpses of the future. In other words, our dreams allow us to handle life.

Unfortunately, many of our dreams are hard to understand. They often contain symbols that need to be interpreted. These symbols can occur in many forms, but animals seem to appear more frequently than any other. This is why animal dreaming has received so much attention throughout the ages.

A lady went to see Carl Jung because she was concerned about a dream she had experienced. Her dream involved a small mechanical animal made entirely of diamonds. In her dream it was alive and moved around. Jung told her: "That is to prove to you that the impossible is possible . . . You are not open to miracles, and there are miracles. In the realm of the psyche, miracles can happen."[3]

Another example of animals appearing in a dream as a symbol of something else occurred to a businessman client of Jungian analyst Fraser Boa. The man dreamt that he went to a large house and saw an exhibition of paintings and drawings of different animals. Then he went to another room where a man asked him what costume he was going to put on, and tried to hand him a painter's smock. The businessman was able to interpret the paintings as symbols for all the writing he should have done. The smock indicated what he should be wearing if he was going to become serious about his writing.[4]

Recurring dreams are also common, and are a sign that an important message is failing to get through to your conscious mind. It pays to think seriously about recurring dreams, as the hidden message is usually vital to your future progress. An acquaintance of mine who is now a successful artist experienced recurring dreams of a flock of geese that were disturbed and became airborne. After about three months, he suddenly realized the geese were trying to motivate him into attempting a full-time career as an artist.

In my late twenties, I had a recurring dream that I can still recall as clearly as if I'd dreamt it last night. In my dream I was walking through a forest in search of a missing kitten. I could hear its plaintive meows, but spent what seemed like hours trying to find it. When I finally found it, I hugged it and felt my heart expand to several times its normal size. I took this dream to be a sign that I should follow the path I truly loved, rather than the career I was pursuing at the time.

Recurring dreams sometimes occur as nightmares, and these can be terrifying. Recurring nightmares are a sign that the person is rejecting important aspects of his or her being. It is important to write down as much as you can remember about recurring nightmares when you wake up. Read what you have written later on in the day and see if you can interpret the symbolism in your dream.

I have met a number of people who remember their dreams well, but cannot remember any animals appearing in them. I think everyone has dreams involving animals at different times, but animal lovers appear to have them more frequently. I have always loved animals, and throughout my life have had a wide variety of animal friends. Consequently, I frequently see animals in my dreams, even if they are merely part of the background.

Just recently, I dreamt of a seaside cottage that we had stayed in for a summer when I was a child. I had not visited this house in more than fifty years, and have no idea why I suddenly dreamt about it. In my dream, I walked up to the front door. As I reached it, the door opened and a large black cat came out. It rubbed itself against my legs and continued into the garden. I walked inside and carried on with the dream. The cat played no further part in my dream, and may have appeared simply because I love animals and expect pleasant places to have animals living in them. However, there may have been a symbolic reason for its appearance, which is why I paid special attention to its appearance in my dream later on.

Most of the time, animals play a strongly supportive role in our dreams. They teach us how to live in a natural, instinctive way, living in the precious now rather than endlessly worrying about things that may never happen. They can teach us to stand up for ourselves, and at the same time make us aware of our true inner natures.

Robyn, a student of mine, came to class extremely excited one evening. The previous night she had dreamt of an eagle, tethered to a railing. Its feathers were bedraggled and it looked beaten and ready to give up. Suddenly it looked up and saw another eagle flying high up in the sky. The tethered eagle visibly grew in size and strength as it watched the other bird. It shook the leg that was tied to the railing, but it was no use. It was tied too firmly. But the eagle looked skyward again, spread its wings, and this time soared upwards. The tie appeared to dissolve as the eagle flew majestically up to greet the other bird.

"That was me!" Robyn exclaimed. "I was that tethered bird. I've been trapped and tied down for years, but now I know I can set myself free. You wait and see!"

That dream magically restarted Robyn's life. She freed herself from a dead-end job and left a relationship that was going nowhere. She returned to college and finished her degree, and the last time I saw her she was planning her first overseas trip. Dreams do have the power to change people's lives.

A businessman I know told me about a dream he had the night before he was due to sign an important contract. Although he'd had doubts about the principal of the other company, he'd ignored them as all the figures stacked up, and the deal seemed to be a highly lucrative opportunity. In his dream, the businessman was hosting a cocktail party. He was enjoying the party until a beautiful woman, dressed entirely in black, walked into the room. She walked directly up to him, and as she drew close, he saw a dozen or more venomous snakes appear from her breasts. He recoiled in horror, and the woman disappeared. The next morning the businessman refused to sign the contract, as he considered the snakes were a warning that everything was not above board.

"That was the only time I experienced a dream of that sort," he told me. "Logic told me to sign the contract, but my feelings told me to let it go. For a while I thought I'd done the wrong thing, but about a year later the company collapsed, and a huge amount of fraud was uncovered. If it hadn't been for that dream, I'd have signed the contract."

Animals often appear in our dreams when we are aware that it is time for a change, but are reluctant to do anything about it. We might feel reasonably contented stuck in a rut, but our animal helpers are not prepared to accept that.

They will keep on appearing and disturbing us until we finally get the message and make some changes.

Christopher had a well-paid job in the computer industry. He had a beautiful baritone singing voice, and at one time had hoped to become an opera singer. After completing a music degree, he decided it was time to do something sensible, and he gained computer qualifications. However, no matter how well he did in the computer industry, or how much money he took home each month, he was aware of an emptiness inside. He also had constant dreams about a goat. In his dream, Christopher would be trying to get the goat into an enclosure. Every time he succeeded, the goat managed to get out again before Christopher could close the gate.

"I was the goat in the dream," Christopher told me. "I was also me, of course. I was trying to put myself into a small square box, but the other me, the goat, wanted freedom, and wouldn't let me. Even the animal was right. Goats are so stubborn, and that describes me to a T. When I finally realized what the dream meant, I gave up my job. I upset everyone—my fiancée, my parents, even my brother. But I'm on track now. I'm going to be an opera singer."

Dream animals can prod us in different ways, teaching us not to take ourselves so seriously.

Humphrey is an accountant who has a wardrobe full of conservative clothes. He has to dress conservatively for work, but even his casual clothes are dull and unexciting. One evening he dreamt about a chicken in his local shopping mall. Humphrey was captivated by the sight of a chicken in such an unlikely place and followed it into a menswear store. While there, he looked at different items of clothing. Each time he did this, the chicken would become agitated and would try to lead him to a display of brightly colored casual clothes. The chicken stopped making a fuss only when Humphrey started looking at these garments. Each time he tried to look at more conservative clothes the chicken became distressed. Finally, mainly to placate the chicken, Humphrey bought some colorful shirts and a sports jacket.

Humphrey thought about his dream the next day, and he understood exactly what it meant. He visited the store in the mall and bought some items of clothing that he would never have considered in the past.

"They are not as bright as the clothes in my dream," he told me. "But they're totally different from anything I've ever bought in the past. And you know what? I feel like a different person when I'm wearing them."

The chicken mischievously brought more excitement and happiness into Humphrey's formerly colorless life.

Dreams involving sick, dead, or abused animals can be disturbing, but they also have messages for us. An elderly friend of mine dreamt about a dead cat every night in the week before he died. Rather than being disturbed by this, he took comfort in the fact that the cat was dead but the cat's consciousness continued to exist. He took this to mean that although he would shortly die, his soul would live on.

Sick and abused animals are an inner part of our makeup telling us that we are sick or abused. Once we realize the situation we are in, we can do something about it.

Felicity was physically and verbally abused by her husband for almost twenty years. It had gone on for so long that she had almost forgotten that it was possible to live without it. One night she dreamt that she was a bear in a zoo. Her keeper constantly abused and tormented her, even when she was sick. Every day she was forced into a sunny enclosure where people could see her, even though she wanted to lie down in the shade to get better. Finally, she died, and it was several hours before anyone noticed.

Felicity woke up in a cold sweat. If she carried on living in the way she had been, one day she'd be dead and it would be ages before anyone noticed. Felicity was too scared to say anything to her husband, but she confided in two friends, and they helped her leave her home and start again.

Everyone dreams, but many people pay no attention whatsoever to their dreams. You would possibly think that these people are missing out on the extra insights that dreams can offer. Funnily enough, this is not always the case. Our dreams come from our subconscious, which works in a different way from our conscious minds. We can think about things endlessly in our conscious minds, but sooner or later have to go to sleep. In our sleep, our subconscious minds can take over the problems and work on them at a deeper level. Frequently, this will solve the problem, and it explains why we can wake up in the morning with the answer to a problem that had baffled us during the previous day. Consequently, our dreams continually work to help us, whether we are aware of this or not. Naturally, we can expect even greater benefits when we start paying attention to our dreams.

Researchers at Harvard Medical School found that sleeping and dreaming after learning new information helps the brain to process new information. Professor Robert Stickgold, who led the study, says, "Dreams are the brain's way of processing, integrating, and really understanding new information. Dreams are a clear indication that the sleeping brain is working on memories at multiple levels."[5]

If you're studying important new information, you'll learn it more quickly, and with greater recall, if you take a nap after the period of study. The Harvard researchers found that people who did this were up to ten times better at the learned task than people who did not go to sleep after the study period.

I keep a dream diary by my bed and record my dreams as soon as I wake up. For many years I wrote down every dream I could remember, but nowadays I only record the dreams that appear significant. These include recurring dreams, dreams involving members of my family, dreams involving animals, and dreams that do not seem to have any immediate relevance. The dream of the summer cottage fits into the last two categories.

By recording my dreams in this way, I have gradually built up a valuable record of what is going on in my subconscious mind. Frequently, I return to my notes and can see how different dreams have helped and guided me in different areas of my life. Sometimes, dreams that made no sense to me at the time become extremely obvious when I read them weeks or months later. A dream diary has been extremely helpful for me, and everyone I know who has adopted the habit has experienced similar results.

However, if you are going to keep a dream diary, make sure to record everything exactly as you remember it. The value of it is lost if you censor what you write. We all dream about things that we would not want others to know about. Everyone experiences sexual, violent, or bizarre dreams from time to time. Just because we dream about strange things does not mean that we would ever consider doing these actions while awake. Record them in your dream diary exactly as you remember them and, if necessary, keep your diary where no one else can read it.

Paying attention to our dreams, and recording them, gives us a valuable opportunity to get to know and understand the desires, needs, suggestions, and predictions of our unconscious minds. This can help us understand our motivations and become more aware of ourselves as complete, rounded people. Once we know and understand ourselves, we can direct our lives in any direction we wish.

As dreaming is something that everyone does every night, most people tend to take their dreams for granted and pay little attention to them. Consequently, it is not surprising that most people quickly forget their dreams shortly after waking up. Fortunately, it is not hard to become better at remembering your dreams.

Before going to sleep, tell yourself that you want to remember your dreams. This alone will help you remember much more. When you wake up, spend a few minutes with your eyes closed, thinking about any dream fragments that are in your mind. As you think about them, more details will come back to you. It might be hard to do this during the week, especially if you jump out of bed when the alarm clock wakes you up. If this is the case, set aside a morning during the weekend to practice this. You are more likely to remember a dream when you wake up naturally. This is because you normally wake up after a REM cycle if it occurs close to your usual waking time. When this happens, you are likely to remember the dream.

As you take more interest in your dreams, you will also become more aware of the symbolism in your dreams. Any time spent thinking about your dreams will be worthwhile. It will help you become more self-aware, and will enable you to understand why you act in certain ways. Examining your dreams can be extremely useful in understanding your motivations and feelings.

Another good reason to keep a dream diary is to confirm the accuracy of your predictive dreams. We all dream about events that have yet to happen, and it can be helpful to discover how common they are. Up to 10 percent of your dreams relate to future events. However, research at the Maimonides Medical Center dream laboratory in New York City indicates that you can increase the number of precognitive dreams you have by telling yourself before falling asleep that you will have dreams about the future that night. Malcolm Bessent, a subject in these experiments, was asked to dream about something that would happen the following day. He did this successfully on fourteen out of sixteen nights.[6]

Unfortunately, most people who experiment with this find themselves dreaming of distressing events in the future. This is possibly because sad or tragic events usually contain more emotion than dreams of other kinds. You can take control of your dreams and eliminate the unpleasant ones, if you wish. Before going to sleep, tell yourself that you will have pleasant precognitive dreams during the night and that you will remember them in the morning.

When you wake up, lie quietly for a few minutes before getting up and think about your dream. Most people remember the last few seconds of their dreams. Gently prod your mind to go back further and further into the dream, until it all returns to your conscious mind.

We'll cover how to remember your dreams in greater detail in the next chapter.

CHAPTER TWO

How to Remember Your Dreams

Everyone has had the experience of remembering a dream when first waking up, only to find it has been completely forgotten a few minutes later. For thousands of years, people have devised different methods hoping they would ensure their dreams were captured and remembered.

The ancient Greeks used special techniques in their dream temples to encourage recall. These included avoiding broad beans and abstaining from sex. The dreamers also underwent ritual washing before settling down to sleep on the skins of animals. The temple of Asclepius at Epidaurus was the most famous of these dream temples. Asclepius was the Greek god of medicine, and if he visited the temple overnight, everyone sleeping there was healed.

You will rarely remember your dreams if you use an alarm clock. This is because an alarm wakes you up with a start, and any dreams that may still be in your memory

will instantly disappear. Consequently, the best time to recall dreams is often during the weekend, when most people
wake up naturally, without an alarm clock. When you first
wake up, lie quietly, without moving, and then gently see if
you remember your dreams. Do not struggle or strain to recall your dreams. If you do, you can almost guarantee that
you'll remember nothing. Simply lie peacefully and quietly
for a few minutes and see what comes into your conscious
mind.

You'll find that as you start paying attention to your
dreams, you'll be able to remember more of them. However, from time to time you'll still experience the frustration
of waking up, knowing you've just had a dream but finding
it already out of reach.

On the following pages are several methods that people have found helpful. No matter which method proves
most useful to you, you still need to record your dream as
quickly as possible, as otherwise it will be forgotten as you
go through your day.

I keep a dream diary beside my bed. This enables me to
record my dreams as soon as I wake up. If I happen to wake
up in the middle of the night with a memory of a dream, I
can quickly jot down a few notes to help me remember it
in the morning. Some people prefer to record their dreams
on a tape recorder or another recording device. A friend of
mine has a pen that contains a small recording device. He
uses this to record any good ideas he has during the day,
and he also keeps it beside his bed at night to recall his
dreams.

Meditation

Meditation is a useful way to relax your body and mind by focusing on an object or thought. Meditating before you go to bed is a good way to ensure a restful sleep and pleasant dreams. Most people meditate in a sitting position, but you can also do it lying down, standing up, or even walking. You might like to meditate in a warm bath before getting into bed. Alternatively, you might like to listen to some gentle and relaxing music before going to bed. I prefer to meditate before going to bed, as I generally fall asleep in the middle of the meditation if I do it in bed. This is not necessarily a bad thing, but I prefer to complete the meditation before going to sleep.

A simple way to meditate is to sit down in a comfortable chair, close your eyes, and take several slow, deep breaths—holding each breath for a few seconds before exhaling. Make sure to hold the breath in your abdomen. As you exhale, allow all the muscles of your body to relax. Once you feel totally relaxed, focus on your breathing. You might like to say to yourself, "In," as you inhale, and "Out," as you exhale. Continue doing this for as long as you wish. When you are ready to finish the meditation, tell yourself three times that you will remember any dreams you may have.

Go to bed as soon as possible after the meditation. If you wish, you can repeat the meditation in bed, and allow it to send you to sleep.

Bathing Ritual

This ritual can be performed at any time but is supposed to work best when the moon is waxing. Add a couple of spoonfuls of salt, or bath salts, to a pleasant, warm bath and relax in it for as long as you wish. While you are in the bath, remind yourself several times that you will be dreaming and will recall at least one of your dreams in the morning.

When you get out of the bath, dry yourself with a good-quality, clean bath towel. Make sure your bedroom is reasonably warm. If you wish, you can light candles, or burn incense or a calming aromatherapy oil to create a pleasant atmosphere in the room. Remember to carefully extinguish them before getting into bed.

Snuggle down between the sheets, remind yourself again that you will remember your dreams, and allow yourself to drift off into sleep.

Positive Expectation

Before falling asleep, say to yourself that you will wake up in the morning with a clear recall of at least one of your dreams. You might need to affirm this several times before allowing yourself to drift off into sleep.

Change of Routine

This method involves changing your sleeping position by sleeping with your head at the foot of your bed. This disorientates you enough to encourage dreaming, and the surprise when you wake up will hopefully help you remember your dream.

An acquaintance of mine took this a step further. His house had four bedrooms, and he slept in a different room each night. He was convinced that this increased his ability to remember his dreams.

Edgar Cayce's Method

Edgar Cayce (1877–1945), the American psychic and healer, believed the body played a part in remembering dreams. Consequently, it was important not to move and to remain in the same position when waking up, until a dream has been fully remembered. Edgar Cayce felt that most dreams were unimportant, and it didn't matter if they were not recorded. However, he also thought that important dreams would be repeated in a variety of ways until the dreamer finally managed to remember them.

Affirmations

Affirmations are short phrases or sentences that are deliberately inserted into the conscious mind. Possibly the most famous affirmation of all was created by the French psychologist and pharmacist Émile Coué (1857–1926): "Every day, in every way, I am getting better and better." Affirmations are always said in the present tense, as if whatever it is that is desired has already occurred. Consequently, someone who was unwell would not say, "I will get better." It is much more effective to say something along the lines of, "I am fit and well," or "I enjoy good health."

An affirmation to help dream recall should be said several times a day. You might use: "I always remember my dreams when I wake up."

Dream Diary

Placing a dream diary and pen on your bedside table subliminally reminds you that you are serious about remembering your dreams. You can take this a step further, if you wish, by removing any distractions, such as a television, from your bedroom, and adding anything that you feel will help dream recall. Some people find that hanging a dream catcher over their bed helps them remember their dreams. Others place a crystal beside the bed or under a pillow.

The biggest advantage of keeping a dream diary is that you gradually build up a collection of dreams that would otherwise have been lost. Some people write something in their dream diary every night, but it is more common to write in it once or twice a week. Reading your dream diary after a month or two helps you notice recurring themes and your emotional reactions to different situations.

You may find a particular animal appears in your dreams on a regular basis. A friend of mine discovered that many of her dreams included a goldfish that swam round and round inside a small bowl. On thinking about this, she realized that it symbolized the emotional restrictions in her life.

When You Don't Remember Your Dreams

The chances are that you'll dream more than 150,000 dreams during your life. Most of them are not important, and it doesn't matter if you don't remember these. Consequently, if you wake up in the morning with no memory of any of your dreams, you should not be concerned, as none of them were especially memorable.

The dreams you are most likely to remember are:

1. Dreams that include strong emotions and feelings.
2. Recurring dreams.
3. Strange and weird dreams.
4. Transitional dreams. These occur when you are contemplating, or making, a major change in your life.

Interpreting Your Dreams

Sometimes the meaning of an animal in your dream will be obvious. However, there will also be occasions in which an animal plays a part, or even a major role, in a dream, and you have no idea why.

Almost always, animals appear in your dreams to offer you guidance, help, and advice. They want you to progress and develop in this incarnation. If you are not sure of the message that has been sent to you in a dream, you can ask yourself a series of questions to try and clarify the situation. You might ask:

Was the animal helpful, supportive, and life-affirming?

Was the animal terrifying?

Did it chase me?

What do I consider to be the main strengths of this animal?

Was the animal wild or tame?

What was the animal doing?

You should also ask questions about your role in the dream, such as:

Was I on my own, with a friend, or possibly in a crowd?

Was I happy, sad, lonely, lost, or searching for someone or something?

Was I actively participating in the dream, or was I simply observing?

Was I the animal?

Which gender was I in the dream?

Was I a child, old, or somewhere in between?

Which other people were involved?

Where did the dream take place?

Relive the dream as completely as possible in your mind, and then write your recollections down as quickly as you can, before the memory fades.

Once you have recorded the dream, you can interpret it. There are a number of ways to do this:

1. If you're a logical person, you'll probably analyze your dream using your rational mind.

2. Use your intuition. After all, the dream came from your subconscious mind, and you can gain valuable insights by tapping in to your hunches and feelings.

3. Discuss your dream with others, and see what ideas and suggestions they have.

4. Write down everything that comes to you. Sometimes thoughts and insights can come to you while you're writing down your dream. You will not always be able to analyze your dream right away, and this is especially the case if it's part of a sequence of dreams that may not yet be complete. Sometimes the meaning of a dream only becomes obvious weeks or months later.

Some people get confused at this point, as they're not sure if the interpretation they've put on their dream is the right one. Fortunately, there are a number of ways to check this:

1. A sense of relief. This is an awareness that the interpretation is correct.

2. A physical response. Your body never lies. If you feel a sensation in your body, such as your heart beating faster or even tears, it's a sign that your interpretation is correct.

3. A sense of knowing. This is an intellectual awareness that the interpretation is correct.

4. A psychic awareness. This is a sense that the interpretation is correct.

It's impossible to remember all your dreams. Recall and record as many of your dreams as you can, but don't worry about the elusive dreams that don't come back to you. If they're vitally important, you'll dream them again and again until you do remember them.

CHAPTER THREE

Animal Symbolism

Most cultures contain elements of animal symbolism, but none have taken it to the extent of the Chinese, with their huge range of diverse animal symbols. Some of these symbols are extremely old and date back to China's prehistory. The variety of different animals is not surprising, as "there is virtually nothing in the whole of nature, organic or inorganic, no artifact, which the Oriental artist does not see as imbued with symbolic meaning."[1] This is why the Taoists frequently use stories of animals to help teach their wisdom.

Symbols are a form of shorthand, in which a glimpse of something as simple as a butterfly can provide a wealth of information. Sometimes these meanings were deliberately hidden, but more frequently the meanings have been lost over the years. Carl Jung defined it well: "A word or an image is symbolic when it implies something more than its obvious and immediate meaning."[2]

The word *symbol* means something that is used to represent something else. For instance, most people would consider a dove to be a symbol of peace and gentleness. Similarly, a lion is considered a symbol of courage. The word *symbol* is derived from the Greek word *symballein*, which means "to join together." Symbols frequently form a chain of associations that date back to antiquity, revealing the major role that symbols have played in the development of humanity. In fact, the most important symbols have always attempted to create harmony and significance in everyday life in a mysterious, and often frightening, world.

Not surprisingly, familiar objects—such as animals, plants, and stones—became symbols. The ancient Chinese watched fish struggle upstream to reach their breeding grounds, often leaping up large waterfalls in the process. Not surprisingly, fish became a symbol of upward progress. Similar examples could be seen everywhere people looked.

Chinese Animals

The most commonly known examples of Chinese animal symbolism are the twelve animals of the Chinese zodiac. However, there is also a bewildering array of other animals that are featured in stories and festivals, and can be found as images almost everywhere, even on items of clothing.

Animal motifs can be found on ancient bronzes dating from as far back as the Hsia Dynasty (c. 2100–1600 BCE). The *Tsao Chuan* (606 BCE) records the answer an emissary made to King Chuang when he asked a question about the animals depicted on some ritual vessels. The reply included the comment that the animals depicted on the vessels were to help people distinguish between good and bad animal spirits.[3]

This spiritual aspect was important, and, as the animal designs contained magical significance, they were considered to be messengers from the spirit world.[4]

The Chinese have charming stories to explain virtually everything, and the origin of the twelve animal signs is no exception. According to legend, the ruler of heaven was the Jade Emperor, and it was he who decided which animals would be included.

The Jade Emperor had never visited Earth and was curious about the different animals who lived there. He asked his chief assistant to gather the animals together and bring them to him. His assistant explained that there were many thousands of different animals, and that it would take months to collect them all. The Jade Emperor thought about this, and asked his assistant to bring him the twelve most interesting animals.

The assistant went down to Earth, thinking about what he should do. He invited the rat to attend a meeting at six o'clock the following morning to meet the emperor. He also asked the rat to invite his friend, the cat. Invitations were also sent to the dog, the dragon, the horse, the monkey, the ox, the rabbit, the ram, the rooster, the snake, and the tiger.

The cat was thrilled to receive an invitation to meet the emperor and asked the rat to wake him up in the morning, because he often overslept. The rat agreed. That night, the rat looked at the cat as he slept. He saw how streamlined and handsome the cat appeared, and the rat became concerned that he would look bad in comparison. Consequently, when he woke up the following morning, he did not wake up the cat, and raced to the meeting on his own. When the rat arrived, all the other animals except for the cat, who was still fast asleep, were already there.

At six o'clock, the emperor came out and inspected the animals. He liked what he saw, but noticed that there were only eleven animals. His assistant was equally as concerned, and ordered a servant to go down to Earth and bring back the first animal he saw.

The servant found himself out in the country. Walking towards him was a farmer carrying his pig to market. He quickly explained his predicament, and the farmer gave him the pig to take up to heaven.

While this was going on, the rat was becoming concerned that he would not be noticed. He jumped onto the ox's back and started playing a small flute. The emperor was captivated by the rat and gave him first place, ahead of all the other animals. Second came the ox, as he had been good enough to allow the rat to jump on his back. Third came the tiger, because he looked strong and handsome. He was followed by the rabbit, because of his beautiful fur. The dragon came next, because he looked just like a huge snake with legs. He was followed by the snake, because of his undulating body. Following him came the horse, because of his composure and bearing, and the ram, because he had trumpet-like horns. The monkey was playful and agile, so he came ninth, and the fine-feathered rooster came tenth. In eleventh place came the dog, because he was faithful and protective, and at the end of the line, in twelfth place, came the pig.

As soon as the animals had been arranged in order, the cat arrived. He pleaded with the emperor to be considered, but it was too late—all the places had been taken. The cat saw the rat standing in the first position and chased him. Ever since that day, cats and rats have been sworn enemies.

Chinese astrology contains many animals in addition to the twelve animal signs. In the Three Lives system of astrology there are another twelve animals, all of whom are highly symbolic. These animals are unusual because although they are all found regularly in Chinese art and literature, they do not—with the exception of the swallow and the pheasant—appear anywhere else in Chinese astrology. The animals in the Three Lives system are the phoenix, the lion, the golden pheasant, the mandarin duck, the swallow, the heron, the stag, the peacock, the pigeon, the sparrow, the eagle, and the white crane.

There are also the animals of the twenty-eight constellations. These are the crocodile, the sky dragon, the badger, the hare, the fox, the tiger, the leopard, the unicorn, the buffalo, the bat, the rat, the swallow, the pig, the porcupine, the wolf, the dog, the pheasant, the rooster, the crow, the monkey, the gibbon, the tapir, the goat, the buck, the horse, the stag, the snake, and the earthworm.

In addition, there are four heraldic animals: the snake, the tiger, the phoenix, and the dragon. The snake is frequently replaced by the tortoise, and the tiger by the bear.

Solely using basic Chinese astrology, we can come up with more than fifty different animals, all of which contain symbolic meanings.

Animal Symbolism in the West

Western astrology also makes use of symbolic animals. Aries has the ram, Taurus the bull, Cancer the crab, Leo the lion, Scorpio the scorpion, Capricorn the goat, and Pisces has two fish swimming in opposite directions. These animals date back to Babylonian times.

Mythology is full of animal references. In Greek mythology, Zeus was able to change his shape into that of a swan, and even a bull, when he approached a young woman he desired. In Germanic mythology, the goddess Freya had a sacred cat. Wotan had his sacred boar, horse, and raven.

Symbolic animals also appear in the Bible. In the Revelation of St. John the Divine (Revelation 4:6–8), we read:

> And before the throne there was a sea of glass like unto crystal: and in the midst of the throne, and round about the throne, were four beasts full of eyes before and behind. And the first beast was like a lion, and the second beast like a calf, and the third beast had a face as a man, and the fourth beast was like a flying eagle. And the four beasts had each of them six wings about him; and they were full of eyes within: and they rest not day and night, saying, Holy, holy, holy, Lord God Almighty, which was, and is, and is to come.

These four beasts from the Bible can be related directly with the four heraldic animals that we have already met: the snake, tiger, phoenix, and dragon.[5] These animals symbolize the Four Heavenly Kings. Taoists believe that these kings control the four spheres of heaven.

Animals have also been used to symbolize people in the Christian tradition. Depictions of eagles, lions, and oxen can be found in many old churches. The lion symbolizes Mark, the ox Luke, and the eagle John. (Matthew is depicted as a man or an angel.) Christ, of course, is usually symbolized as the Lamb of God. However, he is also symbolized as a fish, lion, pelican, unicorn, and as a serpent on the cross.[6] In Christian art the Holy Spirit is frequently represented as a dove. Satan is symbolized by the dragon, serpent, and swine.

Many of the Christian saints are symbolized by animals:

Bear: St. Columba

Boar: St. Emilion

Bull: St. Adolphus

Calf: St. Walstan

Camel: St. Aphrodisius

Cow: St. Berlinda

Crocodile: St. Helenus

Crow: St. Vincent

Deer: St. Henry

Dog: St. Benignus, St. Bernard

Dolphin: St. Adrian

Donkey: St. Anthony of Padua

Dove: St. Ambrose, St. Basil, St. Catherine of Sienna

Eagle: St. Augustine, St. Gregory the Great, St. John the Evangelist

Falcon or Hawk: St. Bavo, St. Edward

Fish: St. Andrew, St. Raphael, St. Simon

Frog: St. Huvas

Goose: St. Martin

Hare: St. Albert of Sienna

Hen: St. Pharaildis

Horse: St. Barochas, St. Irene, St. Severus of Avranches

Leopard: St. Marciana

Lion: St. Adrian, St. Ignatius, St. Jerome, St. Mark

Ox: St. Blandina, St. Luke

Pig: St. Anthony of Egypt

Rat: St. Gertrude of Nivelles

Raven: St. Benedict

Rooster: St. Peter

Serpent: St. Cecilia, The Virgin Mary, St. Patrick

Sparrow: St. Dominic

Swan: St. Cuthbert, St. Kentigern

Wolf: St. Blaise

In the Greek and Roman traditions, various animals were considered sacred to particular deities:

Asclepius: serpent

Apollo: wolf, gryphon, and crow

Bacchus: dragon and panther

Diana: stag

Hercules: deer

Isis: heifer

Juno: peacock and lamb

Jupiter: eagle

Mars: horse and vulture

Mercury: rooster

Minerva: owl

Neptune: bull

Venus: dove, sparrow, and swan

Vulcan: lion

In the Egyptian tradition, three of Horus's sons are shown as animals.

Prehistoric people painted animal pictures on the walls of caves in Africa, France, Scandinavia, and Spain. Some of these were used for sympathetic-magic purposes; in some caves, the animals have been deliberately pitted to indicate a symbolic slaughter. Other animals are depicted mating, showing that these pictures were used in fertility magic.

The Shamanic Tradition

In the shamanic tradition, the spirits of animals have been regarded as teachers and guides for thousands of years. This tradition is universal. In Siberia the spirits of bears were considered of prime importance. Wolves play a major part in the shamanic tradition of North America. Jaguars perform the same role in South America, just as lizards and hawks do in Australia and hares do in Britain. These, and other spirit animals, tell us humans about their knowledge and insights, and allow us to view life in a different way. Whether we are aware of it or not, animal spirits constantly help us. In fact, in some parts of the world it is believed that if we lose contact with our animal spirits we will die.

The Aborigines in Australia are born into a totemic identity, which is usually an animal or plant, but may be something else in nature, such as the wind or water. Consequently, every person belongs to a group of people who share the same totem. Among other things, this ensures stability and harmony within the tribe. Marriages are not permitted between classes, which ensures that people cannot marry someone who has the same totem as they do. (This is common in many tribes in the Native American tradition, also.) This prevents inbreeding, and also means that no totem is more important than another.

People do not eat the flesh of their totem animal. Someone who had the emu as his totem would view the idea of eating emu as akin to eating himself. The relationship between someone and his or her totem provides access to unlimited Earth wisdom, and is lifelong and life-affirming. It gives the person a spiritual identity as well as a responsibility to accept and adopt every aspect of his or her totem.

The Native American tradition also considers nature to be full of spiritual significance. Animals such as the eagle, hawk, owl, otter, deer, and buffalo contain different meanings for different tribes, but the underlying spiritual connection is always present. They are considered spiritual as well as physical beings. All of nature is considered to be the framework in which the spirit and human worlds meet.

The Native American cosmology consists of three worlds: the physical, the subtle or soul, and the spiritual. We, in conjunction with the rest of the animal kingdom, live in all three worlds at the same time. Consequently, when we watch an eagle in flight, we appreciate not only its physical body but also its soul, which gives it life, and its connection with the eternal. We also see it as an archetype of a strong, powerful, soaring, graceful bird. No wonder it is considered such a powerful totem animal.

Animal Spirits

There are a number of ways to look at animal spirits. You might decide, like the Aborigines with their Dreamtime, that they are real spiritual beings who exist to help you whenever necessary. You might choose to think of them as animal archetypes created by your subconscious mind. No matter how you view these animal spirits, you can become so close to them that you will be able to sense, feel, touch, and smell them. You might even be able to temporarily become the animal. This is known as *shapeshifting*. Once you accept spirit animals into your life, you will be able to make use of the animal wisdom that will come to you through your dreams.

There is no need to go out and find your spirit animal. He or she will find you. In fact, you may already have some idea as to who it might be. If you collect miniature elephants, for instance, your subconscious mind is telling you that your spirit animal is probably an elephant. Perhaps you have always been fascinated with foxes, or owls, or turtles. That could well indicate your spirit animal.

Just recently, I was in London and was traveling on the Underground with a friend. He had recently become involved with spirit animals and was searching for his spirit animal. As the train came above ground, he was telling me that he had come to the conclusion that his spirit animal must be a fox as images of foxes kept coming into his dreams. The train came to a gentle stop between stations, while we waited for another train to pass. My friend told me that he had also started seeing foxes regularly. This surprised him, as he had never noticed many before. Suddenly, he laughed out loud and pointed outside the carriage. We were stopped beside a bush-covered slope. Halfway up this slope sat a fox, calmly surveying the train. He looked at the train for some sixty seconds before getting up and disappearing into some scrub.

"See what I mean?" my friend said.

I was as impressed as he was. It was the first time I had seen a fox in the wild, and central London was almost the last place I would have expected to see one. This experience seemed to indicate that my friend's totem animal was a fox.

Oddly enough, a few months earlier I had seen my first raccoon in the wild, while I was on a golf course in Florida. On that day, I was with a woman who told me her spirit animal was a raccoon. As soon as she finished telling me this, the raccoon appeared. Apparently, they are rarely seen in daytime, but this raccoon appeared totally unconcerned about that, or about us. He slowly circled a small area of rough, and then disappeared into it. We went up to where he entered the undergrowth, but he had completely disappeared. It was fascinating to help two people confirm their spirit animals in this way, on two different continents, in the space of a few months.

Some people are surprised to discover that their spirit animals are not the animals they would have chosen themselves. I know a man who has a snow goose as his totem animal.

"I really wanted a lion," Hugo told me, over a cup of coffee. "Lions are strong and powerful. A wolf, or a bear, would have been good, too. A goose is—well—not exactly in the same class as a lion. Anyway, a few months ago I went for a job interview. I was a bit nervous about it and called my goose to me. He came instantly, as he always does. I was walking along the street and suddenly I was inside him. I was the goose! It gave me quite a start, but I felt fantastic. They didn't know it, but the people interviewing me were actually talking to a goose." Hugo smiled. "And I got the job."

Hugo's experience was an example of involuntary shapeshifting. Usually, shamans enter into a trance state before experiencing shapeshifting, but it can occur at other times, usually when the spirit animal decides it is in your best interest. Obviously, this was the case in Hugo's important interview, as he was nervous and stressed. When he called on his goose for support, the goose decided that Hugo would perform better if the two became one.

Instead of getting the animal we want, we tend to get the animal or animals that we need at a particular time. Consequently, you may feel that your totem animal is a wolf, for instance, but then find that a bear or a rabbit starts appearing in your dreams. This means that you should pay attention to the symbolism, meanings, and characteristics of whatever animal or animals you were dreaming about.

In the Native American tradition, valuable life lessons are obtained from animals. Communication with animals is seen as normal and commonplace. In our sophisticated, fast-moving societies we tend to forget that we can communicate with all living things. If you've ever owned a pet, for instance, you will know how the two of you communicated in a variety of ways, both verbally and nonverbally. In fact, many people communicate intuitively with their pets.[7]

How to Find Your Spirit Animal

For some people this process is incredibly easy. They know instinctively who their spirit animal is, and are immediately able to make use of the wisdom and support that their totem animal can provide. Other people find the process more difficult. What follows are a number of methods to help you find your spirit animal. At some level of awareness your subconscious mind already knows who your spirit animal is. When you find it, your subconscious will give a sign of recognition that you will be able to sense.

Dreams

Many people find their spirit animal in their dreams. A certain animal becomes a regular part of their dreaming, and they gradually realize that it is, in fact, their spirit animal making himself or herself known to them. This is different from an animal who appears once or twice in the form of a dream. That animal is likely to be bringing you a message that needs to be interpreted. A spirit animal that appears in the form of a dream will do so regularly rather than occasionally.

Induced Dreams

Induced dreams are dreams that are deliberately implanted into the subconscious mind. They are a highly effective way to help you find your spirit animal. Every night before going to sleep, tell yourself that while asleep you will dream of your spirit animal, and will remember this dream in the morning. Do not blame yourself if this does not work on the first, or even seventh, night. Simply say the same words to yourself every night until you wake up one morning with the dream in your mind.

Lucid Dreaming

Lucid dreaming occurs when you realize that you are dreaming while you are still experiencing the dream. You are physiologically asleep but are consciously aware at the same time. Lucid dreaming was first written about in the West when a Dutch physician, Frederik van Eeden, wrote an article on the subject for the *Proceedings of the Society for Psychical Research* in 1913. Van Eeden found that he could direct his dreams anywhere he wished. Instead of having apparently random dreams, he could turn his dreams into exciting adventures.

The problem with lucid dreaming, though, was that it occurred spontaneously at unexpected times, usually only a few times in the average person's life. Fortunately, a number of methods have been devised to help people have lucid dreams when they want to, rather than leaving it to chance.

Some people find that meditating before going to bed helps them experience a lucid dream when they fall asleep. Shamans know that drumming and chanting create a state of mind that enhances the frequency of lucid dreams.

Interestingly, people who keep dream diaries are more likely to experience lucid dreams than people who don't. This may be because such people place a degree of importance on their dreams that is lacking in those who make no effort to record or analyze their dreams when they wake up.

One method that works well for me is to tell myself shortly before falling asleep that I will experience a lucid dream that night. However, my students have had little success experimenting with this, and I know only a few people who are able to experience a lucid dream using this method.

I have had much more success in helping people by encouraging them to use self-hypnosis to bring about lucid dreaming. The technique is a simple one.

1. Set aside ten minutes during the day in which you will not be disturbed. Sit down in a comfortable chair.

2. Start by taking ten slow, deep breaths. Inhale to a silent count of three, hold the breath for another three, and then exhale to the count of five.

3. Tell yourself that you are relaxing, and allow each part of your body to relax as much as possible.

4. When you feel completely relaxed, say to yourself: "Tonight, while I'm dreaming, I will somehow be-

come aware that I'm dreaming, and will be able to direct my dream anywhere I wish. I'll become aware that I'm dreaming, and will be able to direct my dream anywhere I wish." Repeat these words several times. It is important to say them to yourself with conviction. Any doubt in your mind will make it harder to succeed.

5. When you feel ready to return to everyday life, count slowly from one to five, and open your eyes.

6. When you go to bed, remind yourself that you will be lucid dreaming, and then go to sleep in your usual manner.

Naturally, once you start lucid dreaming, you can take it anywhere you wish. It is best to use your first lucid dreams to do things you have always wanted to do. Once you become familiar with lucid dreaming and feel comfortable with it, you can use it to lead you to your spirit animal.

Several people have told me that the experience was so emotionally charged that they woke up. Other people were surprised at their spirit animal and tried to direct their dream towards another animal. I have even had people tell me that they were initially unhappy with their spirit animal, and repeated the exercise several times over a succession of nights, in the hope that they would be taken to a more preferable animal. This never worked. Each time they returned to the same animal, who was patiently waiting in exactly the same position he or she had been in during the previous dream.

Likes and Dislikes

We all have preferences about different things in our lives. The same thing applies to animals. Many people love cats, but there are others who cannot even stand being in the same room as one. I love monkeys, but my wife considers them unappealing. A neighbor of ours keeps pet rats. I have nothing against rats, but I would never choose to keep them as pets.

My mother loved chickens. When she died, I inherited a third of her collection of ceramic chickens sitting on baskets. I love these chickens, as they contain so many memories, but I would not build up a collection of them myself.

Go back through your own life and see which animals have responded best for you. A collection of animals could be a sign that this is your spirit animal. A school friend of mine always drew pictures of dogs when he doodled. Not surprisingly, the dog is his spirit animal. A relative of mine bought a baby goat as a pet. Before long, she had dozens of them. I was not at all surprised to learn that the goat is her totem animal.

When one of my students did this exercise, she discovered that every time she felt depressed, she saw a robin, and this cheered her up. She did not realize this consciously until she went through her life and discovered how a robin had appeared every single time. The robin is obviously her spirit animal, and she now looks for robins everywhere she goes.

Astrology

Look closely at the animals that relate to you in both Chinese and Western astrology. These animals have a part to play in your life, anyway, and you should think about them quietly and see if they play a more important role than you had thought.

Here are the relevant years relating to the Chinese zodiac:

The Rat: 1924, 1936, 1948, 1960, 1972, 1984, 1996, 2008

The Ox: 1925, 1937, 1949, 1961, 1973, 1985, 1997, 2009

The Tiger: 1926,1938, 1950, 1962, 1974, 1986, 1998, 2010

The Rabbit: 1927, 1939, 1951, 1963, 1975, 1987, 1999, 2011

The Dragon: 1928, 1940, 1952, 1964, 1976, 1988, 2000, 2012

The Snake: 1929, 1941, 1953, 1965, 1977, 1989, 2001, 2013

The Horse: 1930, 1942, 1954, 1966, 1978, 1990, 2002, 2014

The Sheep: 1931, 1943, 1955, 1967, 1979, 1991, 2003, 2015

The Monkey: 1932, 1944, 1956, 1968, 1980, 1992, 2004, 2016

The Rooster: 1933, 1945, 1957, 1969, 1981, 1993, 2005, 2017

The Dog: 1934, 1946, 1958, 1970, 1982, 1994, 2006, 2018

The Pig: 1935, 1947, 1959, 1971, 1983, 1995, 2007, 2019

Remember that the attributes the Chinese give these animals are not necessarily the same as the ones we use in the West. In Chinese astrology, the rat is considered ingenious, charming, and sociable. These qualities are not likely to spring to mind in someone born in the West who is thinking about rats.

Numerology

Numerology is the ancient art of determining someone's character and destiny from the numbers related to their date of birth and name. You can use basic numerology to see which animals relate best to you. There are three important numbers, derived from the person's date of birth and full name at birth, that can be used. These are the Life Path number (from the date of birth), and Expression and Soul Urge numbers (from the person's full name at birth). We'll discuss how to determine and use these numbers in chapter 4.

Pendulum Method

The pendulum is a useful tool that has many applications. It consists of a small weight attached to a thread, cord, or chain. Despite its simplicity, it allows you to perform virtual miracles, as it provides access to your subconscious mind.

Ideally, the weight should be between three to six ounces, and the thread should be three to six inches long. Hold the thread between the thumb and first finger of your right hand and allow the weight to swing freely. (If you are left-handed, hold the pendulum with your left hand.) If you are going to be using the pendulum for any length of time, it is helpful to sit at a table and rest the elbow of the arm you are using on the table.

Stop the movements of the pendulum with your free hand, and then ask the pendulum which direction indicates "yes." It might take a minute or two to respond. Once you become accustomed to using a pendulum, the responses are instant, but it takes time to reach that stage. Once the pendulum starts to respond, it will move either to and fro from side to side; or in a circle, clockwise or counterclockwise. Make a note of the response, and then ask the pendulum which movement represents "no." These are the only two responses you need for the experiment to follow, but you might want to find out which directions indicate "I don't know" and "I don't want to answer." Once you have done this, you can ask the pendulum any questions you wish.

Now you can use the pendulum to determine your spirit animals. Before asking the pendulum to indicate your particular totem animal, make a list of as many animals as possible. Now you can hold the pendulum, and ask it: "Is such-and-such an animal my spirit animal?" The pendulum will answer yes or no. Go through your entire list, even if you receive a positive response early on. This is because it is possible that you have more than one totem animal.

There is something you should be aware of, though. If you have a strong emotional attachment to the answer, the pendulum will give you the response that you desire. Consequently, if you are convinced that your totem animal is a bear, for example, your pendulum will probably agree with you. In cases like this, it is better to ask someone who is not emotionally involved in the answer to hold the pendulum for you.

Meditation

This is a pleasant exercise that can provide surprising answers. Many of my students have found this to be the most successful way of finding their totem animal. It consists of a guided meditation. All you need do is sit or lie down comfortably with your eyes closed, and follow the suggestions in the script.

You might like to make a recording of the script, or perhaps have a friend read it to you. Alternatively, you might prefer to read it through several times to familiarize yourself with the content, and then say it to yourself in your own words while you're relaxing.

Make sure that the room is reasonably warm. You might want to cover yourself with a blanket. Wear loose-fitting clothes, and ensure that you are as comfortable as possible. Then close your eyes, relax, and follow the suggestions. There is no need to try hard. All you need do is relax and listen. It doesn't matter if you drift off into a daydream either. When you become aware that you've stopped paying attention, simply start listening to the voice again.

Meditation Script

"Take a nice deep breath in, and let it out slowly. Allow all those muscles to relax. Each breath you take makes you more and more relaxed. Take another breath, and exhale slowly. Feel that relaxation drifting through every cell of your body. It's so simple and effortless and sooo relaxing.

"Focus on the muscles around your eyes. They are the finest muscles in your entire body. Focus on those muscles and allow them to relax completely. Relax those muscles, and then let a wave of relaxation pass right through your body, from the top of your head to the tips of your toes. It's so easy and so pleasant to be totally relaxed like this, where nothing need bother or disturb you. Allow that pleasant relaxation to reach every part of your body.

"It's so comfortable and peaceful to relax like this, and each breath you take allows you to drift even deeper into this pleasant, relaxed state. You'll gradually find that all outside noises will fade into the distance, more and more, and you'll pay attention only to the sound of my voice as you relax even deeper and deeper.

"So pleasant. So comfortable. And sooo relaxing, as you drift even deeper. You're in a nice, pleasant, peaceful state now, but you can go even deeper into this wonderful feeling of total relaxation. It's so easy to do, and so beneficial for you.

"And now, visualize in your imagination the most wonderful, peaceful scene that you can remember. You can even make up a beautiful picture, if you like. Imagine yourself in this wonderful scene. It's a magnificent day and you feel surrounded by peace, tranquillity, and universal love.

"In your mind's eye, see yourself get up and walk across this beautiful scene. You can see a set of steps, and you're curious to see where they lead. As you get closer, you can see that it's a beautiful, wooden staircase leading down to a small grove of trees. The sun creates a dappled effect on the long grass as it passes through the trees. It smells warm and fresh, and reminds you of pleasant incidents in the past when you communed with nature. The grove looks so welcoming and attractive that you decide to go down the stairs and into this beautiful grove.

"Place your hand on the handrail, and allow yourself to double your relaxation with each step as you go down the ten steps to the grove below. Ten. Drifting down deeper and deeper into pleasant relaxation. Nine. Another step down, doubling your relaxation again. Eight. Almost floating down another step. Seven. Drifting and doubling your relaxation once more. Six. More and more relaxed. Five. Halfway down this beautiful staircase. Four. Doubling your relaxation. Three. So, so deeply relaxed. Two, and one. As you step off onto the nice warm grass you feel so incredibly relaxed, so loose and limp and revitalized in every particle of your being.

"You step into the glade. Right in the center is a beautiful glen, and you lie down in the sunshine, enjoying the feel and scent of the beautiful grass.

"As you lie there, so serene and relaxed, you become aware of small sounds around you. You realize that different animals are sharing this magical glade with you. You feel safe and protected and realize that none of these animals mean any harm. They are naturally curious about you, and in your mind's eye you see different animals coming into the glen to look at you. Some stay a short while, but others stay longer, perhaps sensing the degree of rapport they have with you. Some animals appear again and again, while others come just the once. You notice that this glade shelters hundreds of different animals, and that they all live at peace with one another.

"As you lie there, watching the animals appear and disappear in your mind, you become aware of the special attraction you feel towards some of these animals. You enjoy seeing them all, but there is a special bond between you and certain animals.

"And now it grows quiet and all the animals disappear. You remain calm and relaxed, because you know that in just a few moments you'll see your special spirit animal. Take a nice, deep breath and let it out slowly. Become aware of yourself, lying peacefully in this pleasant oasis, protected, safe, and so, so relaxed.

"As you become aware of yourself and visualize the scene in your mind, allow the first animal you think of to enter into your scene. Observe this animal quietly, dispassionately. This is your spirit animal. Your spirit animal is there to guide and assist you in any way you wish. Take a moment or two to become familiar with your spirit animal."

(Pause for approximately sixty seconds.)

"And now it is time to return to full conscious awareness again on the count of five. You'll open your eyes, feeling wonderfully alive and full of abundant energy. You'll also open your eyes with a variety of insights about your spirit animal.

"One, gaining energy. Two, feeling stimulated, excited, and extremely happy. Three, coming up more and more. Four. Almost there. And five, eyes opening and feeling wonderful."

Dancing

My wife would tell you I'm a shocking dancer. All the same, this is my favorite method to determine totem animals. It is an ancient shamanic method called "summoning the animals." It involves two rattles and movement. If you want to be completely traditional, you can make your own rattles by placing pebbles inside a gourd. Alternatively, you can buy something suitable at a music store. For some years I had a pair of rattles that I found in a toy store. They were brightly colored and made of plastic, but they made a pleasant sound and worked well.

Ensure that you have complete privacy and will not be disturbed for at least half an hour. Wear loose-fitting clothes. Determine the four cardinal directions.

1. Stand in the center of an imaginary circle, facing east. Extend your right arm in that direction and shake the rattle three times. This indicates that you are about to start the dance.

2. Pause for twenty seconds, and then start shaking the rattle in your right hand vigorously. While you are doing this, think of your need to identify your spirit animal.

3. After thirty seconds, turn to the south and shake the rattle for thirty seconds in that direction. Repeat with the west and north. Continue thinking about your spirit animal.

4. Face east again, and this time shake both rattles rapidly. Start to dance on the spot as you slowly turn around in a circle. The movements you make are personal to you. Be as original and creative as you can. Shake both rattles in all four directions. Then shake them upwards towards the heavens, and downwards towards Mother Earth.

5. Continue shaking both rattles, but slow the tempo down slightly. Start moving around the room. You are now waiting for a sign that your spirit animal is

nearby. Sing, call out, or make animal noises, if you wish. Be prepared for anything that your emotions bring to the surface.

6. Reduce the tempo again. Move around the room using the gait of different animals. Soon you'll be guided towards your spirit animal. This will come as a feeling, a sensation, or simply as a sense of knowing. Allow the feeling to build up inside you. Allow your spirit animal to enter your being, so that you become one.

7. Stop dancing, and allow the rattles to fade away once you have full knowledge of your spirit animal and can feel him or her inside you.

8. Spend as much time as you wish welcoming your spirit animal.

9. When you feel ready, face the east again, with your right arm extended. Shake the rattle three times to indicate that the rite is over.

Dressing Up

This method uses the shamanic technique of dressing up as an animal. By doing this you gain the characteristics of the animal. You do not need the animal's coat to do this. Anything that symbolizes or represents the animal will do.

Start by collecting objects that relate to all the animals that appeal to you. Once you have enough items, find a place where you will not be interrupted. Strip down to your undergarments and then attach to yourself an item that symbolizes one of the animals. Sense what it feels like.

Move around the room as if you were that animal. If you wish, make animal noises. See if it feels right.

Take off the items relating to that first animal. Stand up, stretch, and take several deep breaths to remove the energies of that animal from your body. Then do the exercise again, using an item that represents another animal.

Enjoy this exercise. It is supposed to be fun. Laugh at yourself as you imitate the movements and sounds of the different animals. If someone walked into the room and saw you, they would probably laugh. Feel free to laugh at yourself, too.

At some stage during this exercise you will probably feel that one animal is right for you. It will come as a sense of knowing, a gradual awareness that this is your spirit animal. Continue with the exercise until you have tried all of the animals. Before you finish, put on the object that relates to the animal that felt right. Be this animal again, and see if the same sense of knowing comes back to you.

Of course, it's possible that you'll do this exercise and find you make no connection with any of the animals. If this occurs, gather items that relate to other animals and go through the exercise again.

Remember to do these exercises in private. People are more open today than ever before, but there is still the possibility that they will not understand. Rather than upset and confuse others, it is better to perform exercises or rites of this sort privately.

You might be surprised at the spirit animal who appears to you. There is no need to be. Over a lifetime you will have a number of spirit animals, as they come and go as you need them. Most people are not even aware of this happening.

Sometimes they leave because they've been neglected. Once you've found your spirit animal, you need to keep in touch with him or her. Dancing is a highly effective way of doing this. Relaxing and having intuitive conversations together is another. Walking in the sort of environment that your spirit animal would feel comfortable in is another excellent way to initiate communication. A friend of mine walks regularly in a park near his home and considers it the most holy place in the world, as it is here that he can enjoy lengthy, undisturbed conversations with his spirit animal.

Once you've formed a strong connection with your spirit animal, you'll notice his or her presence in your dreams. Although they may not always figure directly in the dreams, you'll be aware of their influence on the content, and will receive valuable messages in your dreams.

In the next chapter we'll take this a step further and look at your personal totem animals.

CHAPTER FOUR

Your Animal Totems

Many people consider human beings to be superior to the other forms of life on our planet. These people have not stopped to consider that all forms of life are important. All living things are the creation of the Universal Life Force that gives consciousness, intellect, and spirit to all of her creations. Appreciation of this helps us recognize the sanctity of nature and enables us to revere all forms of life. The fact that we can learn from other forms of life has been known for thousands of years. There is a wonderful passage in the Bible that demonstrates this: "But ask now the beasts [animals], and they shall teach thee; and the fowls of the air, and they shall tell thee. Or speak to the earth and it shall teach thee; and the fishes of the sea shall declare unto thee" (Job 12:7–8).

Totemism is the belief that a person or group has a mystical relationship with an animal or plant, known as a *totem*. The totem is considered the emblem or symbol of the person or group.

The word *totem* comes from *ototeman*, used by the Ojibwa in the area of the Great Lakes in North America. This word originally meant "brother-sister kin," which signified the blood relationship between siblings. In 1791, a British merchant introduced the word into English. He mistakenly believed the word *totem* meant a person's guardian spirit that appeared in the form of an animal.[1]

Many young Native American men were sent out to find their totem animals. They abstained from food for four days and spent their time asking the Earth Mother and the Power Above to protect them, and to provide them with a spirit helper. During the four days they were away from their tribe, they experienced many visions—no doubt caused by hunger, sleep deprivation, and communication with the gods—before finally finding their totem animals. At some stage during the four days, the young man would see the animal that was going to become his totem. He would kill it with his bow and arrow, and would keep a small portion of it to act as his protective totem.[2]

After this, the totem was considered a companion, friend, protector, and guide. The person symbolically identified himself with the totem animal, and would not kill or eat that animal ever again.

Totemism played a major role in the lives of Native Americans and Australian Aborigines. However, in various forms it has been practiced around the world. In ancient Britain, for instance, the blackbird was considered a messenger of the dead. The Incas respected the condor and the puma, as they believed they were sent from the spirit world. The polar bear served in this way for people in Siberia, and the eland was the principal spirit animal for the San people of southern Africa.

More and more people around the world are becoming aware of the sanctity of all life. Humans are just one form of life on this planet, and we have a duty to look after our environment and all living things. This concept is ancient. The *Bhagavad Gita* (6:28–32) states that people who make contact with the Godhead and lead good, blameless lives become able to see "the Self in every creature and all creation in the Self." This means that we are all one.

So-called primitive people have always been aware of this. They regarded the earth as their mother and considered all life to be their brothers and sisters. Naturally, they killed animals for food, but the concept of killing animals for "sport" was unknown. When the Ainu people of northern Japan killed a bear, they blessed the animal's soul and told it to be reincarnated as an Ainu.[3] The ground was tilled for food, but it was given time to restore itself before being planted again.

It's not hard to imagine what a present-day Aborigine feels when he looks at the site of a huge uranium mine in the formerly pristine Kakadu National Park in the Northern Territory of Australia. For more than a decade people have protested about this mine, which is closed down at present only because uranium prices are low.

I'm using the word *totem* in this chapter for convenience. Your totem animal is an animal that you have a special affinity for, usually because of its attributes or symbolism. In many ways, it could be considered an archetype of your animal inner self. In some cultures, the totem animal is considered an ancestor, or as the physical aspect of a deity. Many people consider their totem animal to be a type of spirit guide. I would be more inclined to call this a spirit or power animal, but I realize that for many people, these are all synonyms for the strength and protection provided by their personal totem.

How to Find Your Totem Animal

Some people instinctively know what sort of animal their totem animal is. Others have to discover their totem animals through experimentation. It is important to have no expectations about who your totem animal is. If you're convinced that your totem animal is a lion, for instance, this preconception may well prevent you from discovering your true animal totem.

Here are several methods that you'll find useful if you're unsure who your totem animal is.

How to Find Your Totem Animal through Name Associations

Years ago, I met a man with the surname of Fox. Not surprisingly, he considered the fox to be his totem animal. Consequently, if your last name happens to be Hawk, Crow, or any other animal, you should seriously consider that animal to be your totem animal.

A woman I knew many years ago spent her childhood years living on Horse Parade Avenue. Probably because of this, her totem animal was a horse. I happened to mention this at a talk I gave, and several people immediately raised their hands. A woman told us that she lived on Monkey Apple Street, and her totem animal was a monkey. A man

said he lived on Bullrush Drive, and his totem animal was a
bull.

How to Find Your Totem Animal through Personal Interests

A friend of my mother's collected statues, photographs, and
paintings of elephants. She did this for many years, without
pausing to wonder why she was so attracted to elephants.
She surprised herself when she realized that the elephant
was her totem animal. If you have a collection of a certain
animal, you should ask yourself why you feel attracted to
that particular animal, as it may well be your totem animal.

How to Find Your Totem Animal through Unexplained Occurrences

If a particular animal keeps appearing in your life, it may
well be your totem animal. This is especially the case if the
animal appears in places where you would not expect to
find it. You would not expect, for instance, to see a hawk
inside a cave. If you receive regular, unusual occurrences
involving the same animal, speak to it telepathically and
find out if it is your totem animal.

How to Find Your Totem Animal through Meditation

The word *meditation* worries many people. For the purposes
of finding your totem animal, all it means is sitting down
quietly somewhere where you will not be disturbed. Close
your eyes and take several slow, deep breaths. Allow all the
muscles of your body to relax. Start with the muscles in your

toes and feet, and gradually relax all the muscles in your body.

When you feel totally relaxed, ask yourself who your totem animal is. Wait and see what comes into your mind. You may receive a clear impression of a particular animal right away. However, it is more likely that nothing much will come to you, and your mind will gradually think about other things. When you discover your mind drifting, ask the question again, and again, if necessary. Don't worry if nothing comes to you the first time you experiment with this. Repeat the exercise regularly until your totem animal makes himself or herself known to you.

How to Find Your Totem Animal in Your Sleep

One of the most effective ways to find your totem animal is to tell yourself before falling asleep at night that you want to hear from your totem animal. You may not hear from your animal on the first, or even fourteenth, night, but in time you will. You should also remain alert during your normal, everyday life. You may find yourself thinking about a particular animal and realize that this is your totem animal. You can also ask your totem animal to appear to you in a dream. If you request a lucid dream, you'll be able to feel the energy of the animal as you communicate with it.

If this method appeals to you, use whatever aids you feel are necessary to ensure a good night's sleep. You might hang up a dream catcher to symbolically help you dream. You might enjoy a warm bath before getting into bed. You might place a small amount of an essential oil, such as cedarwood, orange, or helichrysum, on the soles of your feet to encourage dreaming. Ylang ylang and vetiver can be used when you wake up to encourage dream recall. Essential oils should always be diluted with a vegetable-based oil to avoid possible irritation to the skin. You should be able to buy essential oils in a diluted form. If you dilute them yourself, you should have approximately 3 percent essential oil to 97 percent base oil.

How to Find Your Totem Animal through Prayer

If you pray on a regular basis, you are likely to find this method useful. Towards the end of your prayers, ask for your totem animal to become known to you. Finish your prayers in your usual manner and carry on with your usual, everyday activities. Continue making this request every time you say your prayers until you discover who your guardian animal is.

How to Find Your Totem Animal Using Character Traits

Another method is to think about the animals you are drawn to. Ask yourself if any of these animals behave in a manner similar to you. Are you mischievous? Your totem animal might be a monkey. Are you quiet and shy? Your totem animal might be a deer. Your personality might provide the necessary clues to tell you who your totem animal is.

How to Find Your Totem Animal Using Astrology

Some people use the animals associated with their horoscope sign. Consequently, an Arian, for instance, might choose a ram as his totem animal. This method is not 100 percent accurate. I knew a Leo who thought the lion would be his totem animal. He gradually discovered his totem animal was actually a polar bear. As four of the zodiac signs are not associated with an animal, this method doesn't work for everyone. Here are the signs that are associated with animals:

Aries: ram

Taurus: bull

Cancer: crab

Leo: lion

Scorpio: scorpion

Sagittarius: horse, as the symbol is half man, half horse.

Capricorn: goat

Pisces: fish

Another method is to use the animals associated with your Chinese zodiac sign. These are determined by your year of birth. The animals associated with each year relate to the characteristics and personalities of the people born during that year. The animals for each year are listed in chapter 3.

How to Find Your Totem Animal Using Numerology

Numerology is an ancient form of divination and character analysis that interprets the numbers derived from people's names and dates of birth. In numerology there are four main numbers: the Life Path, the Expression, the Soul Urge, and the day of birth.

The Life Path

The Life Path represents the person's purpose in life. It reveals what he or she should be doing in this lifetime. The Life Path is determined by creating a sum out of the person's date of birth, and reducing it down to a single digit. Unfortunately, there are two exceptions. If, in the process of reducing the numbers, the total happens to be an 11 or a 22, you do not reduce these to a single digit. In numerology, 11 and 22 are considered Master numbers. Many people think these indicate the person is an old soul.

Here is an example, for someone born on April 28, 1980:

$$
\begin{array}{ll}
4 & \text{(month)} \\
+\ 28 & \text{(day)} \\
+\ 1980 & \text{(year)} \\
\hline
=\ 2012 & 2 + 0 + 1 + 2 = 5
\end{array}
$$

This person's Life Path number is 5.

You may wonder why we create a sum to determine this, as in this case we get the same result if we add the numbers up in a line: 4 (month) + 2 + 8 (day) + 1 + 9 + 8 + 0 = 32, and 3 + 2 = 5. This works most of the time, but Master numbers can be lost when adding the numbers up in a line. Here's an example. A good friend of mine was born on February 29, 1944:

$$
\begin{array}{rl}
2 & \text{(month)} \\
+ 29 & \text{(day)} \\
+ 1944 & \text{(year)} \\
\hline
= 1975 & 1 + 9 + 7 + 5 = 22, \text{ a Master number.}
\end{array}
$$

If we add up her numbers in a straight line, however, we lose the Master number: 2 (month) + 2 + 9 (day) + 1 + 9 + 4 + 4 = 31, and 3 + 1 = 4.

The Expression

The Expression indicates the person's natural abilities. It is derived from all the letters in the person's name at birth, converted into numbers using this chart:

1	2	3	4	5	6	7	8	9
A	B	C	D	E	F	G	H	I
J	K	L	M	N	O	P	Q	R
S	T	U	V	W	X	Y	Z	

Here is an example using an imaginary person named Samantha Jane Courtland.

S A M A N T H A   J A N E   C O U R T L A N D

1 1 4 1 5 2 8 1   1 1 5 5   3 6 3 9 2 3 1 5 4

       23   12   36

    2 + 3 = 5   1 + 2 = 3   3 + 6 = 9

5 + 3 + 9 = 17,
and 1 + 7 = 8

Samantha has an Expression number of 8.

The Soul Urge

The Soul Urge number indicates what the person would secretly like to achieve. It is determined by adding up all the **vowels** in the person's full name at birth.

Unfortunately, there is again one exception. The letter *Y* is a consonant only if it is pronounced. Most of the time it is considered to be a vowel. In the name Yolande, for instance, the *Y* is classified as a consonant, but in Kaye it is considered a vowel.

SAMANTHA JANE COURTLAND

```
 1   1      1   1  5    6 3      1
       3          6            10
                          1 + 0 = 1
```

$3 + 6 + 1 = 10$,
and $1 + 0 = 1$.

Samantha's Soul Urge number is 1.

Day of Birth

The day of birth is the day of the month the person was born on, reduced to a single digit. Because 11 and 22 are Master numbers, someone born on the 11th, 22nd, or 29th of the month does not reduce his or her day of birth to a single digit. 11 and 22 stay the same, and 29 is reduced to 11.

Here are a few examples. If someone was born on the 6th of any month, his or her day of birth number is 6. Someone born on the 16th of any month would have a day number of 7, as 1 + 6 = 7. Likewise, someone born on the 28th would have a day number of 1, as 2 + 8 = 10, and 1 + 0 = 1.

Meanings of the Numbers

Now that you know how to determine the four most important numbers in numerology, it's time to find out what they all mean. Each number has a meaning that reveals the person's strengths and weaknesses.

One

Keywords: Independence and attainment

People who have a one as one of their four main numbers are pioneering, innovative, and entrepreneurial. They possess good minds and leadership qualities. This means that they usually rise to the top position in their field. Ones also have strong personal needs that need to be met.

Some Ones find it hard to stand on their own two feet and achieve independence. They become dependent on others, and are frequently taken advantage of by others.

Two

Keywords: Cooperation and adaptability

People who have a two as one of their main numbers are able to make other people feel at ease. They are gracious, charming, and find it easy to make friends. They are diplomatic, tactful, and naturally intuitive. Because Twos are not overly concerned about status and wealth, they are often found in the "number two" position, rather than as "number one."

Occasionally, someone with a two as one of the main numbers in his or her chart will try to become a leader. Even if this person succeeds, he or she will not be comfortable or happy in this role.

Three

Keyword: Self-expression

People who have a three as one of their main numbers need to express themselves in some way, ideally creatively. This includes singing, dancing, talking, and writing. They are excellent communicators and are usually positive people who express all the joys of life.

Some Threes are superficial dabblers. Their lack of purpose means they waste their lives in frivolous activities.

Four

Keywords: System and order

People who have a four as one of their main numbers are patient, dependable, reliable, hard-working, and well organized. They enjoy working to set routines and gain satisfaction from seeing the results of their hard work. They are good with details and enjoy working on projects they consider worthwhile. They possess a rigid approach to life and find it hard to change their mind once it has been made up. Consequently, Fours are often accused of stubbornness.

Some Fours dislike the necessity to work hard, and become lazy and abusive.

Five

Keywords: Freedom and variety

People who have a five as one of their main numbers are enthusiastic, curious, and versatile. They enjoy travel, excitement, and new activities. They are quick thinkers who become restless and impatient whenever they feel restricted in any way. They remain forever young at heart.

Some Fives overindulge in a variety of ways, and find it hard to stick to anything for long.

Six

Keywords: Home and family responsibility

People who have a six as one of their main numbers are nurturing, caring, and responsible. They enjoy helping others and frequently provide a shoulder for other people to lean on. They are the members of the family that others turn to when things are going wrong. Sixes are sympathetic, kind, and loving. Consequently, they enjoy good relationships with their family and friends.

It is rare to find people using their six negatively. However, a few accept everyone else's responsibilities and end up overwhelmed with all the problems and difficulties.

Seven

Keywords: Analysis, understanding, and wisdom

People who have a seven as one of their main numbers seek answers to the mysteries of life. They enjoy time on their own to grow in knowledge and wisdom. They have their own unique way of doing things. This gives them originality, but it also makes it hard for them to adapt and feel comfortable as part of a group. Sevens usually prefer to have one or two close friends rather than a large group of acquaintances. They are reserved, introspective, and cautious. They are spiritual people who develop a philosophy of life that grows and develops as they mature.

Some Sevens find it impossible to get close to others, and become increasingly introspective and eccentric.

Eight

Keywords: Material freedom

People who have an eight as one of their main numbers enjoy being involved in large-scale enterprises, and want to reap the rewards of their success. They are ambitious and enjoy achieving their goals. They are good judges of character and possess significant leadership potential. They are money-oriented, but can be generous once their own financial needs have been met. Although Eights are rigid and stubborn, they seldom see these qualities in themselves.

People who use their eight negatively can achieve great wealth, but they do it at the cost of health, happiness, and personal relationships.

Nine

Keyword: Humanitarianism

People who have a nine as one of their main numbers are natural humanitarians. They are sensitive, caring people who enjoy helping others. They frequently give much more than they receive back in return. Consequently, other people sometimes take advantage of them. Nines are romantics at heart and are deeply hurt when their love is not reciprocated. The humanitarian ideals of Nines are universal in scope, and they feel a need to help humanity as a whole.

Many people use their nine negatively. They resent remaining selfless and constantly giving to others. Some try taking instead but find that this provides no satisfaction, as it goes against their true nature.

Eleven

Keyword: Idealism

People who have an 11 as one of their main numbers are idealistic, intuitive, and caring. They come up with unique ideas, which need to be evaluated carefully as they're not always practical. Elevens are dreamers and visionaries. However, they frequently find it hard to make their dreams a reality. There is always a degree of nervous tension associated with the number 11.

Because 11 is a Master vibration and difficult to work with, many Elevens become impractical dreamers who achieve little. In their world it's hard to separate fantasy from reality.

Twenty-two

Keyword: Master builder

People who have a 22 as one of their main numbers are able to achieve anything they set their minds on. Elevens are frequently dreamers. Twenty-twos are also dreamers, but have the ability to make their dreams a reality. They are practical, hard-working, constructive thinkers. They are frequently charismatic and unorthodox. They have the ability to motivate and inspire others. They have visions of a perfect world and enjoy working for the benefit of humanity as a whole.

Some Twenty-twos are selfish and use their considerable abilities for their own ends, ignoring the needs of others.

Even if they are aware of this, they find it hard to use their abilities in a more positive fashion.

How to Find Your Totem Animal Using Your Four Main Numbers

Your totem animal is likely to share at least one of your four main numbers. You find this out by converting the name of the animal into numbers, and comparing these numbers with your personal numbers. A lion, for instance, is:

LION

3965

By adding up all the numbers, and reducing them down, we find that the lion has an Expression number of 5, as 3 + 9 + 6 + 5 = 23, and 2 + 3 = 5.

The lion also has a Soul Urge number of 6, as 9 + 6 = 15, and 1 + 5 = 6.

If you have 5 or 6 as one of your four main numbers, the lion would be a good possible choice for you as your totem animal.

Here's an example. Let's assume that Jane Diana Smith was born on June 14, 1983. We start by working out her main numbers:

$$
\begin{array}{r}
6 \\
+\ 14 \\
+\ 1983 \\
\hline
=\ 2003
\end{array}
$$

As 2 + 3 = 5, Jane has a Life Path number of 5.

JANE	DIANA	SMITH
1 1 5 5	4 9 1 5 1	1 4 9 2 8
12	20	24
3	2	6

Jane has an Expression number of 11, as 3 + 2 + 6 = 11.

Jane has a Soul Urge of 8, as the vowels in her name add up to 26, which reduces down to an 8. (1 + 5 + 9 + 1 + 1 + 9 = 26, and 2 + 6 = 8.)

Consequently, Jane's four main numbers are:

Life Path: 5

Expression: 11

Soul Urge: 8

Day of birth: 5

The number 5 occurs twice in Jane's four main numbers. It is reasonably common for someone to have two numbers the same, and this adds power to that particular number. It is less common for someone to have three numbers the same. It is possible, although rare, for the same number to appear four times.

The best totem animal for Jane would have an Expression or Soul Urge number of 5, because it occurs twice in her numbers. She may also choose a totem animal that contains an 11 or an 8.

If you have four different numbers in your makeup, your Life Path represents 40 percent of your makeup, your Expression 30 percent, your Soul Urge 20 percent, and your day of birth 10 percent. Consequently, it is more beneficial for you to choose an animal that has your Life Path number as its Expression or Soul Urge, rather than your day of birth number.

The one exception to this is your Soul Urge number. The best possible combination is for you and your totem animal to share the same Soul Urge number.

Here are some possible totem animals for Jane:

Snake: Expression number of 5

Bear: Expression number 8

Dog: Expression number 8

Albatross: Expression and Soul Urge numbers 8

Bull: Expression number 11

Alligator: Soul Urge number 8

Crocodile: Soul Urge number 8

Rhinoceros: Soul Urge number 8

Tortoise: Soul Urge number 8

Beaver: Soul Urge number 8

Eagle: Soul Urge number 11

Lion: Soul Urge number 11

Horse: Expression and Soul Urge number 11

Jaguar: Soul Urge number 11

Weasel: Soul Urge number 11

Hen: Soul Urge number 5

Elk: Soul Urge number 5

These are just a few of the many possibilities Jane could choose from. The best way for her to decide on her personal totem animal is to write down all the animals that appeal to her. Once she has completed this, she can work out the Expression and Soul Urge numbers for each animal, and decide which one relates best to her.

In the list above, several animals share the same Soul Urge number as Jane. She should examine them particularly carefully to see if any resonate particularly well with her. However, sharing the same Soul Urge number isn't everything, and she might, for instance, decide she'd rather have a horse as her totem animal. In this instance, her Expression number of 11 relates well with the horse's Expression and Soul Urge numbers (both 11), making this a good choice for her.

Sometimes, people find it hard to choose a single animal from the list, and decide they must have a number of animal totems. Everyone has just one totem animal. The other animals are animal guardians. They are willing to help you but act more as guides than as totem animals. If you find it hard to limit yourself to just one animal, take as much time as necessary to gradually determine which one is your totem animal.

Your Totem Animal Can Change

It's possible that your totem animal will change to reflect what is going on in your life at a particular time. A number of animals could come and go over a period of time. You may find you have one totem animal that remains with you no matter what. However, it's just as likely that you have a number of animals at different times.

Once you have discovered your totem animal, you can start communicating with it mentally. You may feel strange doing this initially. In time, though, you'll find that the responses you receive, also in your head, come not from you but from your totem animal. The answers you receive should prove useful and helpful.

Your animal totem gives you an intimate connection to nature. Establishing a kinship with your spirit animal is rewarding for you and, as a bonus, is also good for the world. Once you determine your spirit animal and start working with it, you have a duty to find out everything you can about your chosen animal. Observe your animal if possible. You may have to visit a zoo to do this, but be aware that you are watching the animal in an artificial environment. Consequently, it may not act in the same way it would in its normal habitat.

If you observe your totem animal in the wild, make sure that you are protected. Read books about your animal's folklore. Study its zoology. Ask its spirit to help you learn and understand everything you can. Spend time meditating and allow yourself to become as one with your animal spirit. This will ensure that you do not anthropomorphize your spirit animal. It is an animal, not a human being in disguise.

Some people have an instinctive knowledge of who their spirit animal is. Others have to discover it through dreams and other exercises. Some find it accidentally.

After author Joel Rothschild's best friend Albert Fleites committed suicide, Joel became aware of hummingbirds around him at different times.[4] He took these hummingbirds to be a signal from Albert that death is not the end, that his friend was contacting him from the other side. This may be the case, but it's also possible the hummingbird was Joel's spirit animal and was there to comfort and help him.

In the next chapter we'll look at shapeshifting, which is the art of transforming yourself into an animal.

CHAPTER FIVE

Shapeshifting

Shapeshifting is the ability to transform oneself from human to animal form. Throughout history, shamans have been able to enter into a trance state and transmogrify themselves in this way. They induce trance by chanting, drumming, dancing, rapid breathing, and sleep deprivation. In some cases, especially in the Amazon River basin, psychotropic drugs are used to help reach the desired state. Often the shamans dress themselves with animal pelts, feathers, or antlers to help with the process. Figurines that depict shapeshifters in action have been found in the Balzi Rossi caves in northwestern Italy. They are believed to date back 25,000 years.[1]

Apuleius (second century CE), the Roman writer and satirist, was charged with using magic to secure the affections of a wealthy widow whom he married. His *Metamorphoses*, better known as *The Golden Ass*, includes a fictional account of a witch who shapeshifts into a crow. After burning incense, saying a magic spell, and rubbing her body with oil, wings and a beak appear. The witch then makes a number of crowlike calls and flies out the window. A witness to this occurrence tried to do the same thing, but uses the wrong oil and turns into an ass.

In Europe, people believed that witches had the ability to shapeshift into their "familiar," an animal that helped and protected the witch. These were usually toads, hares, magpies, ravens, cats, dogs, foxes, or goats. In 1627, Richard Bernard wrote in his *Guide to Grand Jurymen* that witches "have ordinarily a familiar, or spirit, in the shape of a man, woman, boy, dog, cat, foal, fowl, hare, rat, toad, etc. And to these spirits they give names."

In 1673, a witch named Ann Armstrong claimed that Ann Baites, also a witch, "hath been severall times in the shape of a catt and a hare, and in the shape of a greyhound and a bee, letting the divell see how many shapes she could turn herself into. They [the witches] stood all upon a bare spott of ground, and bid this informer sing whilst they danced in severall shapes, first of a haire, then in their owne, and then in a catt, sometimes in a mouse, and in severall other shapes. She see all the said persons beforementioned danceing, some in the likenesse of haires, some in the likenesse of catts, others in the likenesse of bees, and some in their owne likenesse."[2]

The Inuit people of Canada believe that in the past humans and animals lived together and were able to freely shapeshift into each other.

In Guatemala and Honduras, the indigenous people had a totem animal known as *nagual*. According to a sixteenth-century Spanish writer, people were able to shapeshift into their nagual animal. If they were injured while in animal form, the same wound would appear in their human body. If the nagual was killed, the person who had shapeshifted into it would also die. Nagual animals were usually deer, dogs, eagles, lions, and tigers. A popular legend says that during the first battles against the Spanish, the naguals of the chiefs were serpents. The highest chief's nagual was a huge green bird. Pedro de Alvarado, the Spanish general, killed this bird with his lance. As the bird died, so did the chief.[3]

Shapeshifting also appears frequently in the Celtic tradition. According to myth, when the Celts first arrived in Ireland the Druid poet Amairgen recited a poem that referred to his shapeshifting experiences:

I am the Wind that blows over the sea;

I am a wave of the Ocean;

I am the Murmur of the billows;

I am the Ox of the Seven Combats;

I am the Vulture upon the rock;

I am a Ray of the Sun;

I am the fairest of Plants;

I am a Wild Boar in valour;

I am a Salmon in the Water;

I am a Lake in the plain;

I am the Craft of the artificer;

I am a word of Science;

I am the Spear-point that gives battle;

*I am the God that creates in the head of man the fire of
thought.*

*Who is it that enlightens the assembly upon the mountain, if
not I?*

Who telleth the ages of the moon, if not I?

Who showeth the place where the sun goes to rest, if not I?[4]

There are many legends about Taliesin, the greatest of
the Welsh bards. This is one that occurred before he was
born as Taliesin. Ceridwen, an evil witch, had an ugly son.
She decided to give her son the gift of prophecy to make
up for his unfortunate appearance. She prepared the necessary ingredients and heated them in a steaming cauldron. A
small boy called Gwion stirred the brew.

As the mixture started to boil, three drops of precious
knowledge splashed out of the cauldron, and Gwion swallowed them. Immediately after this, the cauldron broke,
and Gwion, realizing the witch would kill him, ran away.
He turned himself into a trout and dived into a river, but
Ceridwen changed into an otter and pursued him. Gwion
turned into a hare, but Ceridwen became a greyhound
and continued her pursuit. Gwion became a sparrow, but
Ceridwen changed into a hawk. Finally, Gwion turned himself into a grain of wheat. Ceridwen changed into a black
hen and swallowed the grain.

Nine months later, Ceridwen gave birth to a beautiful baby boy. Ceridwen knew the baby was Taliesin, and
couldn't kill him as he was so beautiful. Instead, she placed
him into a black bag and set him adrift on a river. A prince
found the baby and realized there was something special

about the little boy. Indeed there was, as the baby grew up to become Taliesin, the greatest bard in all of Wales.

In one of the stories in *The Cattle Raid of Cooley*, an ancient Irish epic, two swineherds shapeshift into bulls, ravens, stags, warriors, water monsters, demons, and even aquatic worms. In the same epic, Cúchulain, an Irish mythological hero, is opposed by the Morrigan, a war goddess. In the guise of a beautiful young woman, she tries to make him fall in love with her, without success. She is furious at this, and tells him she will oppose him in his next battle. She changes into an eel that trips him up as he is crossing a stream. She then becomes a wolf that causes cattle to stampede across the stream, and finally she shapeshifts into the heifer that leads the stampede. Each time, Cúchulain wounds her. Once the battle is over, the Morrigan appears again in the guise of an old woman milking a cow. She has wounds in the various places that Cúchulain had injured her in her animal forms. She offers Cúchulain three drinks of milk. Each time Cúchulain blesses her, and after the third blessing her wounds are all healed.

There are many versions of an old European legend about a beautiful young woman called Melusine. In one version, she agrees to marry a young nobleman named Raymond on the condition that he never watch her bathe. The marriage is a happy one, and they are blessed with triplets. One day, Raymond can no longer restrain himself and spies on Melusine in her bath. To his amazement, he discovers his beautiful wife has turned into a sea serpent, with scaly wings and a long tail. Melusine senses her husband's presence, screams, and flies away. She never returns, but the children's nurses tell him that a ghostly figure with a serpent's tail visits them in bed every night.

Other versions of this story say she shapeshifted into the form of a mermaid, a water spirit, or became half woman, half serpent. In some accounts she has no wings but possesses two tails. However, every version involves some form of shapeshifting.

Animal Possession

Lycanthropy is the term used to describe the transformation of a person into a wolf. The belief that a person can, under special circumstances, transform himself or herself into an animal is extremely old. The story of Jove being so angry with Lycaon at serving human flesh at a feast that he turned him into a wolf dates back to Roman times. Virgil, Ovid, Pliny, and Herodotus all wrote about men being transformed into animals. The sagas from Norway and Iceland also tell how men transformed themselves into animals, sometimes by merely donning the skin of an animal.

Transformation from man to animal has always been a rare phenomenon, which is why an article in the October 1918 issue of *The Cornhill Magazine* created a huge amount of interest, and was reprinted in the *Journal of the Society for Psychical Research* in July 1919. The article, "The Hyenas of Pirra," by Richard Bagot, deals with the killing of Nigerian natives while they were in the form of hyenas. The story begins with soldiers noticing that raiding hyenas who had been wounded by gun traps could be tracked to a certain point, where the tracks ceased and were replaced with human footprints. Every time a shooting occurred, a man died in the village, but Europeans were always denied access to the body.

An officer, one Captain Shott, reported an amazing instance in which the tracking began immediately after a hyena had been shot. The men found the jaw of a hyena lying near a pool of blood in a clearing. They lost the tracks when the paw prints reached a path heading to the village. The next day, natives came to Captain Shott and told him that he had shot a village elder called Nefada, and that his jaw had been shot away. The natives had spoken with Nefada shortly before he entered the bush, and later, after hearing a gun shot, saw him return with his face muffled up, appearing unwell.

A number of explanations for this strange occurrence have been suggested. Richard Bagot, the author of the article, thought that the metamorphosis was caused when small black ants created a gravel patch in the ground. He had been told by Italian officials and big game hunters that the native people in Somaliland and Abyssinia considered it extremely dangerous to sleep on ground thrown up by ants. They felt that this exposed the person to the possibility of being possessed by a wild animal, and that once this occurred, the person could never fully escape, and every now and again would temporarily become this animal.[5]

One early researcher into hypnosis, Colonel Rochas, found that he could cause the astral double of a hypnotic subject to form the shape of her mother. If astral doubles can change form in this manner, possibly they could also change into the shape of an animal. Of course, in this instance they would become phantom animals, and research would have to be done to determine if a phantom can be hurt, and transfer that damage to the physical body.

In 1933, Dr. Gerald Kirkland, a Welsh doctor who had been a government medical officer in Southern Rhodesia, attended a ceremony in which he "could almost swear to it that two natives transformed themselves into jackals."[6] The natives achieved this transformation after eating rancid meat and drinking large quantities of alcohol.

In Africa there are numerous accounts of men who transformed themselves into lions and tigers so they could attack and kill their enemies. The Anyotos were believed to drag young girls from their huts at night, and lacerate their backs with knives shaped like leopards' claws. They would then pierce their hearts with a trident-shaped knife, and eat the bodies.[7]

In West Africa, people who were able to temporarily transform themselves into leopards, or possibly even exchange souls with them for a brief time, were known as leopard men.[8]

The Naga people, who live in the hill country between Assam and Burma, believe they can involuntarily project their soul into a lion or tiger, while retaining their own physical form. If an injury occurs to the animal, the human experiences the same injury. The Nagas believe they possess external souls that can roam freely in dreams and may be captured by evil spirits. A temporary loss of the soul is of no importance, but if it travels to the Land of the Dead, the person dies.

Different communities of Naga people have slightly different beliefs on this subject. The Lhota Nagas believe that every medicine man is a leopard-man or tiger-man, but the animal does not receive the medicine man's soul. The Sema Nagas believe that anyone can become a leopard-man. However, it is not a desirable thing to become, as the man is regularly exhausted by the activities of the leopard. Also, the leopard-man is abused if the leopard kills an animal belonging to someone else. Usually, the man's soul will leave while he sleeps, and return before he wakes. However, sometimes it will spend two or three days at a time inside the leopard. The man will go about his normal work, but will be lethargic and incoherent.

A British civil servant, J. H. Hutton (1885–1968), became interested in the subject of leopard-men while working as a subdivisional officer in Mokokchung, a town in Nagaland, in far northeastern India. One day, the village elders came to him asking for permission to tie up a certain man while they were hunting a leopard who had been causing trouble. The man pleaded not to be tied up. It was not his fault that he was a leopard-man. It was not a decision he had made for himself, and he did not want to be one. However, he assumed that the leopard side of himself had to kill in order to eat, and if he did not eat, both of them would die. If he was tied up, and the leopard killed, he would die, too, and the result would be murder.

After a lengthy discussion, Hutton gave the men permission to tie up the man, but said that if the man died as a result of the leopard's death, the person who had speared the leopard would be tried for murder, and would undoubtedly be hanged. When they heard this, the men decided not to tie up the man.[9]

In Malaysia it was believed that people could change into an animal, unconsciously and involuntarily. Although a physical change could happen while the person was awake, the person was usually asleep when his soul transmigrated into an animal. There have also been reported incidents, in both Burma and Indonesia, when entire villages of people were transformed into animals.[10]

In India it was believed that eating certain roots could transform a person into a tiger.[11] In Cambodia, people believed that eating a particular variety of wild rice would have the same effect.[12] The Cambodian version was the more frightening, as it was believed that a man would retain his human mind while in the body of a tiger, but would never be able to change back into human form. Obviously, the combination of a human mind and tiger's body made for an extremely sly, wily, and clever hunter.

There are many dangers in being able to turn yourself into an animal. Not the least of these comes from fellow humans. J. B. H. Thurston related what happened to a traveling salesman in the 1930s in what is now Malaysia. The salesman was traveling between two villages when he heard the roar of a tiger. Naturally, he was terrified, and ran along the track until he came to a large tiger trap. He jumped into this trap and tripped the door so it slammed shut. Shortly afterwards, the tiger arrived and sniffed around the cage but was unable to get in. The tiger eventually gave up and went away.

The salesman found himself trapped in the cage, either unable to get out or perhaps too scared to extricate himself because the tiger was probably still close by. In the morning, a large group of heavily armed villagers came to the trap. Because the entrance was closed, they thought they had captured a tiger. The salesman shouted that he wanted to get out, and told them his story. However, they did not believe him. They recognized him from his previous visits to their village, but said that each time, after he left, a tiger had killed one of them. Around the trap were tiger footprints, but inside the trap were human prints. Obviously, the salesman had got into the trap as a tiger to eat the bait, but had then turned back into a human. Despite the salesman's desperate pleas, the villagers hacked him to death.[13]

One young woman in Malaysia had a narrow escape when she married a man named Haji Ali. He appeared to be a perfect husband in every way. However, one morning he entered the house as a tiger and slowly transformed himself back into human shape in front of his wife. She immediately returned to her parents' home. A few weeks later, someone shot and injured a tiger. The tiger's tracks led to Haji Ali's house, and a pool of blood was found underneath it. Haji Ali, and his two sons from a previous marriage, left the area and disappeared. He was later seen by people who had known him, and they reported that one of his arms was crippled.[14]

In many parts of the world it is believed that if someone is killed and eaten by a tiger, that person will return as a were-tiger. Fortunately, tigers are generally timid and prefer to avoid people. However, attacks do occur, and a number of amulets have been devised to repel tiger attacks. In the Sudan, for instance, people swing a ceremonial knife in the air to repel potentially dangerous animals. In Malaysia, charms are recited to keep tigers away. In addition, a tune can be played on a two-stringed bamboo harp to make any nearby tigers sleepy.[15] Amulets in the shape of tigers and parts of tigers' bodies—such as a tooth, nail, or piece of skin—have also been used as protective amulets.

As you can see, genuine shapeshifting is an extremely rare, and potentially dangerous, phenomenon. I have included it as many people temporarily transform themselves into animals while dreaming. There is no danger in this, of course, and these dreams often provide valuable insights that could not be learned any other way. In fact, these dreams often provide healing. The healing power of animals is the subject of the next chapter.

CHAPTER SIX

The Healing Power of Animals

My mother spent the last three years of her life in a private hospital. She had had a brain-stem stroke, and most of the time was unaware of what was going on around her. However, every day she had two visitors who cheered her up immensely. These were a Labrador dog and a Siamese cat who belonged to people who lived close to the hospital. The dog usually did his rounds in the morning. He would visit every room in turn. The patients who were well enough to speak and pat him did so, but he spent equal time with the patients who were bedridden or unable to talk. The cat visited the patients in the late afternoon. She was more selective, visiting some of the patients but not all of them. Some days, she'd nestle down and fall asleep on one of the patient's beds. Over the course of a week or so, the cat would visit everyone.

All of the patients looked forward to these visits, and some were extremely proud when the cat chose to sleep on their beds. The staff encouraged these visits, as they knew how beneficial they were to all the patients.

Twenty years ago, when this occurred, it was a relatively unusual practice, but today there are many therapy animals that are trained to visit nursing homes and hospitals to provide company and therapy for their patients, both children and adults. Animals are also being used to raise the self-esteem of children with special needs. Special programs, such as Riding for the Disabled and Dolphin-Child Therapy, have been developed to help children who are physically challenged or emotionally damaged.

None of this would be strange to anyone who has had a pet. Pets have been shown to lower stress, reduce blood pressure, provide friendship and support, alleviate depression and loneliness, and provide many other benefits.

Everyone is familiar with seeing-eye dogs that enable blind people to lead fulfilling lives, but few people know that seeing-eye dogs have been used for at least two millennia. A two-thousand-year-old wall painting from Herculaneum shows a blind man, with a dog on a lead, being offered food by a young woman.[1] Although many woodcuts dating from the Middle Ages show blind people being led by dogs, there are no records of dogs being specifically trained for this purpose until the eighteenth century. A painting by Jean-Baptiste-Siméon Chardin called *The Blind Man of the Quinze-Vingts* was hung in the Louvre, in Paris, in 1753. This painting, now lost, showed a patient of the Quinze-Vingts Hospital being led through the streets of Paris by a guide dog. Fortunately, an engraving of this painting still survives. This hospital was established to care for the blind, and trained guide dogs as part of their service.[2]

Animals also help people recover from major traumatic events, such as the death of a partner. An interesting survey in Japan found that people over the age of sixty-five who had a pet visited a doctor 30 percent less often than people of the same age who did not have a pet.[3]

The healing power of animals has been known for a long time. The ancient Greeks used dogs in their healing temples. Florence Nightingale (1820–1910) advocated the use of companion animals to help people regain their health. In 1792, William Tuke (1732–1822), an English philanthropist, started using animals to help improve the conditions, and mental well-being, of people suffering from mental illness. Since 1867, birds, cats, dogs, and horses have been used to help epileptics in Germany.

In 1975, R. A. Mugford and J. G. M'Comisky, two researchers in the United Kingdom, conducted an interesting experiment with twenty-four pensioners. Twelve of them were given a caged bird, while the others received a potted plant. Three months later, the people who had been given a bird had a more positive outlook on life and a better attitude towards others than the people who had been given a plant. In 1980, a study of people with heart disease found that pet owners were much more likely to be alive one year later than people without a pet.[4]

If you have a pet, you'll know exactly how healing and supportive they can be. Pets listen empathically, and respond to your body language and thoughts. Their healing energy takes away pain and hurt. Stroking and cuddling your pet while telling him or her your concerns increases the beneficial effects. If you need healing of any sort, spend quality time with your pet, and allow him or her to give you all the healing energy you require.

Pet owners frequently dream about their pets. It's highly likely that your pet dreams about you, too. Researchers at the Massachusetts Institute of Technology (MIT) discovered that animals experience lengthy and complex dreams that relate to their everyday lives.

Matthew Wilson, an associate professor of brain and cognitive sciences at MIT's Picower Institute for Learning and Memory, and graduate student Kenway Louie taught trained rats to run around a circular track to receive a food reward. The rats' brain activity was monitored while they were running and while they were asleep. The researchers discovered that the rats' brains created a unique pattern of neurons in the area of the brain related to memory.

They then examined more than forty REM (rapid eye movement) episodes while the animals were sleeping. Most dreams occur, in both animals and humans, in the REM state. In about half of the REM episodes that were monitored, the rats duplicated the same brain activity that they had exhibited while running around the track. In fact, the similarities were so close that the researchers were able to determine exactly where on the track the rat was in the dream, and if he or she was running or standing still.[5]

Your pet can provide healing energy while you are asleep, as well as when you are awake. Even if you don't have a pet, you can still use the healing energies provided by the animal kingdom in your dreams. Before you go to sleep, think of a particular animal that symbolizes healing for you. It needs to be an animal you empathize with. Visualize the animal as clearly as you can. Tell yourself that you will experience, and remember, any dreams you may have during the night that involve the particular animal you have chosen. If you have a pet, you'll probably choose him or her. However, you can choose a completely different animal if you wish. If your pet is a goldfish, for instance, you might choose a cat or dog instead.

When you wake up in the morning, lie quietly for a minute or two without moving, and see what dreams come back to you. If you are fortunate, you'll remember a dream that involved your chosen animal. This is unlikely to occur the first time you try it, and most people need to keep visualizing the animal for about a week before the animal appears in their dreams. It is, of course, possible that the animal appeared in dreams you did not recall, but because you specifically asked for a particular animal and also asked to remember the dream, you are likely to remember it when it occurs.

As well as animals you know, or can visualize, you can also experience healing totem animals and animal spirits in your dreams. You can ask them to visit you in your dreams whenever necessary. Most of the time, they'll appear in your dreams before you've asked them, as your subconscious mind already knows exactly what you need.

Part Two

CHAPTER SEVEN

Dream Animal Dictionary

The information in this chapter comes from many sources. I started collecting information on animal symbolism more than forty years ago, and over the years I've recorded what I've learned in a series of notebooks. This was purely for my own benefit, and I had no intention at the time of ever publishing it. My interest in the animals that appear in dreams increased when I was in Hong Kong ten years ago. At the same time, I became fascinated with the animal symbolism of the East. I've also read extensively on the subject, and am blessed with several friends who share this interest with me. Many of the interpretations in this chapter are the result of late-night conversations with good friends, and other people, who were kind enough to tell me about their experiences.

The descriptions and interpretations given here are intended to act as triggers to help you develop your own symbolic meanings. The description of a particular animal might seem uncannily accurate for one person, but not feel right for another. This is because we're all different. Spirit animals share their knowledge and guidance with us in different ways, also, and this can create different shadings of meanings. There is a profound spiritual relationship between human beings, nature, and the archetypal worlds. The purpose of these descriptions is to give you something to think about and to provide a starting point, which you can use to build your own symbology upon.

If the same animal appears in several dreams over a period of time, it may well be your animal totem. This is especially the case if the animal appears in your dreams to help you make the right choices and decisions.

However, the animals you see in your dreams are not necessarily your totem animals. Freud believed that dream animals frequently represented authority figures, including our parents. They can also be associated with primitive drives and instincts that we manage to repress in everyday life. They may also happen to be in your dream because you are dreaming about something that naturally includes animals. If you dream about a zoo, for instance, it would be surprising not to see a large number of animals. If you had a number of pets while you were growing up, any dreams you have about childhood would probably also include animals.

Animals can also symbolize feelings that you may not want to express in your everyday life. If you dream of an angry animal, for example, it could be a sign that you are repressing these feelings in your daily life.

Conversely, if you dream of a happy, carefree animal, it might be a sign that you should be more playful and adventurous in your own life.

Animals can give us important information about ourselves. Just recently, a friend told me about an unusually vivid dream he'd had. He and his wife are expecting their first child shortly. Until now, their "baby" has been a beautiful Airedale dog. My friend dreamt that he was enjoying a walk through a park with his dog. He knew that it was his dog, even though, in the dream, the dog was a golden Labrador. The dog ran ahead, and a minute later my friend heard it howl with pain. He ran to it and found the dog had somehow gashed its shoulder. He cuddled the dog, and then picked it up and carried it home. My friend is looking forward to becoming a father. The dog symbolizes the love, devotion, and protectiveness he'll feel towards the baby when it arrives. The dog was injured and had to be carried home. This demonstrates my friend's sympathetic, caring nature.

The dog in this dream is not necessarily his totem animal. As my friend loves dogs and has owned a number of them over the years, it's not surprising that a dog figured in this dream. The dream was initiated by his feelings about becoming a father, and the dog was the most appropriate way for his subconscious mind to express these feelings.

Consequently, you need to think about the animals you see in your dreams to determine what effect, if any, they have on your life. Dream animals can represent different aspects of the dreamer, but this is not always the case. It's important to examine the particular animal or animals that appear in your dreams and to pay attention to your feelings and reactions to them, as these can influence the interpretation considerably.

Before looking at individual animals, we'll look at some other possibilities and the symbolism attached to them.

Other Symbolism

Animal and Cub

It's an indication that your nurturing qualities are going to be required if you dream of an animal with its cub (or any other offspring). The nurturing can appear in many ways. It may be parental responsibilities. You may be mentoring or helping someone. You might be involved in a philanthropic project. You might be encouraging someone to realize his or her full potential.

Baby Animals

Baby animals in a dream usually relate to the child you used to be. It's a sign that you must let go of the past, become more mature, and face the future with confidence. The interpretation is different for pregnant women. Dreaming of baby animals relates to your feelings for the new life growing inside you. It indicates feelings of love and a desire to bond with your unborn baby.

Pets

If a past or present pet appears in your dream, it's usually a sign of your love and affection for the animal. However, if you don't have a pet, and don't particularly want one, the presence of a pet shows that you, or someone close to you, need some emotional petting and pampering.

Domestic Animals

Domestic animals in a dream show that you have recognized certain qualities in yourself and are making good use of them. The animal may give you solid, practical advice that you can use. Domestic animals also show that you shouldn't make life too complicated for yourself. You might need to take time out to relax and unwind.

Agricultural Animals

As agricultural animals are neither pets nor wild animals, they symbolize qualities that you possess and usually keep under control.

Wild Animals

Wild animals indicate danger, and are usually found in nightmares rather than dreams. If you see any ferocious, angry animals in your dreams, it's a sign that you are anxious about something. You will need to try to resolve the situation.

Taming an Animal

If you are taming an animal in your dream, it's a sign that you're dealing with your subconscious fears, doubts, and worries. You need to nurture yourself more, and refuse to take on more responsibilities than you can easily handle.

Threatening Animals

The presence of a threatening animal in your dream is a sign that a person or situation is causing problems in your life. Think the matter through and decide how threatening or difficult the situation is. Gradually resolve the situation by moving forward one step at a time. Refuse to become involved in any retaliatory action.

Attack by a Wild Animal

It's a sign that you are suffering from criticism, jealousy, and envy if you dream that a wild animal is attacking you. You may or may not be aware of this on a conscious level.

Fear of an Animal

If you are fearful or terrified by an animal in your dreams, it's a sign that you are unsettled by your own thoughts, feelings, and desires. If you are hiding from the animal or feel trapped, it's a sign that your innermost urges and desires are threatening to override your normal, everyday actions.

Wounded Animals

If you dream of a wounded animal, it's a sign that you've been hurt emotionally or spiritually. Take time out to nurture yourself and to reassess where you are going in life.

Caring for an Animal

If you're involved in caring or looking after an animal in your dream, it's a sign that you have been ignoring your own needs while taking care of others. Spend time relaxing and thinking about your life. Decide on something that you'd really like to do, purely for yourself, and then do it.

Eating an Animal

If you find yourself eating an animal in your dream, it's a sign that you're obtaining strength from an outside source, such as a friend or colleague. This strength may also be a result of study or insight into a particular matter.

Prehistoric Animals

It's a sign that some trauma from your distant past, possibly early childhood, is still causing problems for you if you dream of a dinosaur or some other prehistoric creature. You will need to determine exactly what the trauma was and forgive yourself and everyone associated with the event, so you can get on with your life.

Imaginary Animals

It's not uncommon to dream of imaginary animals, such as a unicorn or phoenix. You might even dream of imaginary animals that have no name, because they are unique to you. See if you can understand the needs of the particular animal and see how it relates to you.

Recurring Dream Animals

If the same animal appears regularly in your dreams, it's a sign that either it is your totem animal or you have not yet utilized all the information that the animal has to offer. Remain receptive and open, and start taking small steps forward. Understand and accept that the animal will continue appearing in your dreams until you have learned the lessons the particular animal is willing to teach you.

Dreaming That You Are an Animal

If you dream that you are an animal, or possibly part animal, it's a sign that the characteristics of this particular animal are important to you. If you dream you are the same animal on a number of occasions, it's an indication that this animal may be your totem animal.

Animal Dictionary

Aardvark

The aardvark is an unusual looking nocturnal animal that can grow up to six feet in length. It has the nose of an anteater; a long, sticky tongue; the ears of a rabbit; tough, thick skin; powerful claws; and short, stubby legs. Their teeth continue to grow through their lives. Aardvarks live on ants and termites and can eat up to half a million of them at a time. They are solitary animals who ignore fellow aardvarks except when mating.

In recent times, the term *to aardvark* has become a slang term for having sexual intercourse, possibly because their long tongues search deep inside termite mounds for their nourishment.

Dreaming of an aardvark is a sign that you are performing well but need to move out of your comfort zone. It's a sign of new interests that will take time to master, but will provide enormous satisfaction and pleasure.

Albatross

The albatross is a large oceanic bird. Because albatrosses can glide for days at a time, sailors believed these birds could sleep in the air. In his poem "The Rime of the Ancient Mariner," Samuel Taylor Coleridge (1772–1834) fostered the myth that it is bad luck to kill an albatross. In fact, sailors regularly caught and ate them. In his diary entry for February 5, 1769, written as he was circumnavigating the earth aboard the famous HMS *Endeavour*, naturalist and botanist Joseph Banks (1743–1820) wrote that he "was well enough to eat part of the albatrosses shot on the 3rd, they were so good that everybody commended and ate heartily of them, although there was fresh pork on the table."[1]

Some people still believe that an albatross is the reincarnation of a drowned seaman. Albatrosses can live up to sixty years, but they have become endangered since they breed slowly.

To dream of an albatross is a sign of a large problem or burden that needs to be attended to. This relates to the old saying about "an albatross tied around my neck." Everyone experiences conflicts, worries, financial pressures, relationship problems, and other concerns. If these are not dealt with, they become oppressive and can ultimately affect physical, mental, and emotional health. The presence of an albatross is a sign that you can ignore these problems no longer.

Alligator

Alligators and crocodiles are the largest reptiles in the world. They are also the most dangerous. In ancient Egypt, the crocodile was deified and worshipped as Sebek. It was also related to Ra, the sun god.

To dream of a crocodile or an alligator is a sign that you are involved in an intense, extremely difficult, but short-lived situation. Although it is not necessary, you're likely to take the matter personally. It is sometimes a sign that you need to act quickly and intensely to eliminate the problem.

Dreaming of an alligator or crocodile can also indicate an almost hidden, negative side of your nature that could drag you down and ruin your reputation if you fail to control it.

Ant

The Bible says, "Go to the ant, thou sluggard; consider her ways and be wise" (Proverbs 6:6). Aesop's fable, "The Ant and the Grasshopper," tells how the grasshopper, who had been lazy throughout spring and summer, had to visit the ants to beg for food in winter. Ants have always been considered busy, persistent, thrifty, and well organized. Consequently, to dream of ants is a sign that you are using these attributes to enhance your life. However, knowing this may not give you much satisfaction, as you probably take these skills for granted. Take time to appreciate yourself and think about your special skills and talents. Be aware that your positive nature, industriousness, diligence, and patience will pay off in time.

If the ants in your dream seemed unpleasant, it's a sign that you need more variety and stimulation in your life.

If you dream of flying ants, it's a sign that you are confused and have no idea where you're going in life. This can be extremely disorienting. Nero, the Roman emperor, experienced a number of dreams in which he was chased by swarms of flying ants. This occurred shortly before he became mad, and continued after he had murdered his mother.[2]

Anteater

Anteaters are toothless mammals native to Central America. They can be found between Mexico and Argentina. Anteaters have tubular muzzles and long, sticky, wormlike tongues that help them collect ants and termites for food.

Dreaming of an anteater shows that you have the ability to sense problems and resolve them before they become obvious to others. If something has been lost, dreaming of an anteater is a sign that the lost object will soon be found.

Antelope

The antelope is native to Africa and parts of Asia. They have powerful, long legs and can run and leap fast when necessary. They use their horns as weapons, especially when competing for mates. Their keen senses of hearing, smell, and sight help them to avoid predators.

Dreaming of an antelope shows that you have the potential to act quickly and can even leap over obstacles, when necessary.

Ape

In dreams, apes can indicate that you need to be more flexible in a particular situation. They can also indicate that you need to pay more attention to your physical body. This includes physical fitness, but is mainly concerned with paying attention to your body and listening to what it has to tell you. You also need to avoid acting impulsively at this time.

See also MONKEY.

Armadillo

The armadillo is a small mammal that is encased in a hard, leathery shell. Although armadillos look as if they are totally enclosed in their scalelike armor, the underside of their bodies is covered with fur. Armadillos have sharp claws that they use to dig for food and to create dens for themselves. They have poor vision and short legs. All twenty species of armadillo are native to the Americas. They are amongst the oldest of animals, as they have survived for almost sixty million years.

Dante Gabriel Rossetti (1828–82), the English poet and artist, kept two armadillos as pets. One of them burrowed its way into his next-door-neighbor's kitchen, convincing her that she'd seen the devil.

It's a positive sign to dream of an armadillo, as it shows you are protected from harm everywhere you go. It also shows that you possess empathy and understanding.

Ass

See DONKEY.

Badger

Badgers are quietly determined and persistent. You also possess these qualities if you dream of a badger. It shows you're prepared to stand up for what you believe in, and will work steadily and persistently until you achieve whatever it is you're after. It also shows that you will quietly "badger" someone into action.

If in a dream a badger attacks you, it symbolizes someone who is deliberately hurting you in some way.

The Chinese word for badger is a homophone of a word meaning "to be happy." Consequently, for the Chinese, dreaming of a badger is a portent of pleasant, happy times. If the badger is accompanied by a magpie (as it frequently is in Chinese art), it is considered a sign of great happiness and contentment.

See also MAGPIE.

Basilisk

The basilisk (also known as a *cockatrice*) is a mythical animal that has the head and claws of a bird, and the body of a serpent. It was considered the king of serpents, and it could kill anyone with a mere glance. In Europe it used to symbolize lust, depravity, illness, and disease. Its gaze would kill anyone unwise enough to look into its eyes. In Christianity, the basilisk was a symbol of the devil.

Dreaming of a basilisk is a sign that you're being tempted to do something you know you should not do. Whatever it is, it goes against your essential nature, and you'll be disgusted with yourself if you succumb to this temptation.

See also SERPENT.

Bat

Bats are the only mammals that possess wings. They live in caves and symbolize the unknown. As caves were thought to be doorways to the next world, bats were believed to be immortal. Since they wake up at night, bats also have sexual connotations. To dream of a bat or bats is a sign that you should trust, and act on, your intuition. It indicates a potential for spiritual or mystical growth.

If the bat in your dream appeared frightening, it is a warning that you need to investigate a situation or person more carefully before becoming too involved.

Although the bat has a sinister reputation in Western folklore, in the East the bat is considered highly auspicious and is one of the major indicators of good luck. This is because the word for both "bat" and "good fortune" in Chinese is pronounced *fu*. In Chinese art, five bats are often shown together to symbolize the five blessings of longevity, wealth, health, love of virtue, and a painless death.

In the East, to dream of a bat is a sign of good fortune coming. The more bats in the dream, the better the good luck. It's a sign of incredible joy and happiness when five bats are seen together in a dream.

Bear

Bears were worshipped in prehistoric times, not only because of their strength but also because people believed they were ancestors to mankind. Bears have both positive and negative interpretations in your dreams. If you dream of a good-natured bear, it's a sign that you are gathering your strength and energy so you can accomplish a monumental task. Many people dream that a bear is menacing or chasing them. If this appears in a woman's dream, it's a sign that past hurts are causing difficulties in current relationships. In a man's dream, it's a sign that feelings of inadequacy, dating from childhood, are holding him back.

In Chinese symbolism, the bear symbolizes male energy. (The snake symbolizes female energy.) Consequently, the bear is a symbol of courage, strength, and hard work. If a woman dreams of a bear at around the time of conception, it is considered that she will give birth to a boy.

To dream of a bear indicates a need for the dreamer to cultivate his or her inner strength and courage. The dreamer is likely to have many obstacles that need to be faced, but also has the power to overcome them.

See also PANDA and POLAR BEAR.

Beast

In a dream, a beast is an animal that you cannot identify. Usually, beasts appear in nightmares, and they are so terrifying that the dreamer wakes up in a cold sweat. Beasts are always large and threatening animals that symbolize parts of our nature that have been repressed or concealed.

Beaver

Beavers are industrious, practical animals who create dams and dome-shaped lodges for themselves, sometimes on a grand scale. There is a beaver dam on the Jefferson River, near Three Forks, Montana, that is 2,140 feet long. Most of it is less than six feet high, but parts of it are fourteen feet high and twenty-three feet wide at the base.[3] Beavers work quickly, and can cut down a tree with a six-inch diameter in less than sixty minutes. They can stay underwater for up to fifteen minutes and can gnaw wood while submerged.

Beavers were often considered holy animals in the Native American tradition, able to convey insight and wisdom to the dreamer.

As beavers work cooperatively together, if you dream of a beaver it's a sign that you need to work well with others if you want to progress. Beavers are capable of changing their environments. For this reason, dreaming of a beaver can also indicate that you need to be creative and search for new and fresh ways of doing things.

Bee

An old legend says that Jupiter, the supreme god of Roman mythology, was nourished by bees. However, bees are universally considered a symbol of industriousness, thrift, and dedication. They also symbolize activity, productivity, social organization, teamwork, and cleanliness. To dream of bees is a sign that teamwork, or cooperative effort, is required. If you do this, you will achieve much more than you would be capable of on your own. It's also a sign of multitasking. It's common to dream of bees when you're undertaking something momentous and important, such as an examination, a wedding, or childbirth. Dreaming of a single bee is a sign that you have many good friends.

There is a negative side to dreaming about bees. They can indicate an enormous amount of mindless internal chatter that makes it hard for you to focus and think clearly.

In China the bee also symbolizes a young man in love, and the flower the bee circles (usually a peony) symbolizes the girl he loves. Consequently, to dream of a bee or bees indicates love, romance, and marriage. However, to dream of a bee and a butterfly together indicates sexual intercourse.

A famous dream dating back more than three hundred years relates bees to prosperity. A prostitute regularly dreamt that she slept with a scholar called Mr. Thin Loin. One night she dreamt that after the two of them had made love, Mr. Thin Loin grew smaller and smaller and ultimately turned into a bee. She looked after this bee, which attracted thousands of other bees. The prostitute began collecting and selling the honey, and became rich as a result. For this reason, in China, dreaming of bees is a sign of coming prosperity.[4]

Beetle

More than 40 percent of the named insects in the world are beetles. There are more than 350,000 different species of beetles. Arguably, the most famous beetle of all is the dung beetle, the sacred scarab of ancient Egypt that was thought to push the sun over the horizon every morning. Because the sun rises and sets, the scarab became associated with death and resurrection. This daily renewal offers hope, no matter how dire the situation may be. Consequently, dreaming of a beetle is a sign that the future looks brighter than the present, and a positive attitude and hard work will make it a reality.

Bird

Because most birds can fly, they are thought to symbolize the higher self, as well as creating a connection between the physical and spiritual worlds. It's usually a positive sign for a bird or birds to appear in your dreams, as it means your conscious and subconscious minds are in tune with each other. This can aid spiritual progress. In addition, birds that are flying indicate ambition, freedom, and limitless possibilities. Birds are also able to look at the world from high in the air, and this "bird's-eye view" enables them to assess a situation at a glance.

A single bird relates to increasing independence, and shows that you are, or shortly will be, in control of your life. A flock of birds relates to working and cooperating with others. A bird kept captive in a cage is a sign that your creativity and emotional life are also being held captive.

Dreaming of birds that are squabbling or fighting is a sign of a family dispute or disagreement. The situation needs to be handled carefully to avoid long-term problems.

A bird or birds attacking you in your dream is a sign that other people are attacking your ideas and suggestions. This could take the form of constant criticism and an unwillingness to listen to what you have to say.

Dreaming of a bird building a nest is a sign of partnership, fertility, desire for parenthood, and creating a home. If the bird is leaving the nest, it's a sign of independence and a desire to progress.

See also ALBATROSS, BLUEBIRD, BUZZARD, CANARY, CHICKEN, CRANE, CROW, CUCKOO, DOVE, DUCK, EAGLE, FALCON, GOOSE, HAWK, HUMMINGBIRD, IBIS, KINGFISHER, KIWI, MAGPIE, NIGHTINGALE, OSTRICH, OWL, PARROT, PEACOCK, PELICAN, PENGUIN, PHEASANT, PHOENIX, QUAIL, RAVEN, ROBIN, ROOSTER, SEAGULL, SPARROW, STORK,

SWALLOW, SWAN, TOUCAN, TURKEY, VULTURE, and WOODPECKER.

Bison

Two hundred years ago, the North American bison herds were estimated to be fifty miles long and twenty miles wide. By 1890, only 635 bison remained. Fortunately, there are now approximately 350,000 bison in North America, and as their meat is highly nutritious, most of them are farmed for food. The American bison is very frequently called a "buffalo," even though bison are not closely related to the true, oxlike buffaloes of the Old World. Dreaming of a bison is a sign that you have tremendous power that you have not yet managed to tap and use productively. Spend some time thinking about what you want to do, and once you have worked it out, use your strength and stamina to make it a reality in your life.

See also BUFFALO.

Bluebird

Bluebirds symbolize happiness and a positive attitude towards life. Consequently, to dream of them is a sign that you're achieving your goals and creating the life you desire. To dream of bluebirds is usually a sign that you're currently happy and enjoying life. However, they can also indicate the need to develop a positive approach to life if you are currently unhappy or unwell.

Boar

See PIG.

Buffalo

Buffaloes symbolize strength and power. Lao-Tzu, the philosopher and author of the *Tao-te-Ching*, is said to have ridden a buffalo westward. Buffaloes are usually a positive symbol in dreams. It is a sign that you should return to your roots where you will find satisfaction and fulfilment. A friend of mine became a musician after dreaming of a buffalo. He had spent twenty years working in the computer industry, and returned to music, his first love, after several dreams involving buffaloes.

It is especially auspicious to dream of a white buffalo calf. This is a strong indication that this is the right time to move forward and achieve your dreams.

It's a sign that someone or something is intimidating you if you dream of a herd of stampeding buffalo. Use your strength and courage to stand up to the situation, and it will quickly pass.

See also BISON.

Bull

Bulls are famed for their strength, stubbornness, and aggression. Consequently, they're always associated with masculinity. They can also indicate instinctive urges, as well as an important, powerful person in your life. If a man dreams of a bull, it could indicate a desire to become more aware of the masculine side of his nature. A bull can also indicate the masculine side of a woman's personality.

Bulls can also relate to the old saying, "Taking the bull by the horns." This means overcoming your anger and aggression, and taking control of your life.

An attacking bull is a common dream, and can be a warning that someone is trying to undermine you in some way. Dr. Joseph L. Henderson, a prominent Jungian, recorded a dream told to him by a female patient. In her dream, an angry bull was chasing her. When she realized it was impossible to outrun the bull, she fell to her knees and started to sing to it. The bull immediately stopped chasing her, and even licked her hand with his tongue. Dr. Henderson interpreted this as a sign that in the future the woman would relate to men in a more confident, sexual, and feminine way than she'd been able to in the past.[5]

The sacrifice of a bull has always been considered a sign of victory and success. The Persian sun god Mithras sacrificed a bull to demonstrate the victory of man's higher nature over his primitive animal passions. If you kill a bull in a dream, it's a sign that you're gaining mastery over your baser instincts, and are becoming more mature and responsible.

To dream of two bulls fighting is a sign of disharmony between different members of the family, usually siblings.

See also COW and OX.

Butterfly

The fragile, short-lived butterfly is a symbol of love and beauty. In the East, it is thought that a dead wife may appear to her grieving husband in the guise of a butterfly. The butterfly can also indicate a love relationship between two older people. In Japan, the butterfly symbolizes a young girl turning into a woman. In China, it is associated with the joy and happiness of a young man in love.

To dream of a butterfly is a sign of a long life, surrounded by love and beauty. A butterfly may appear in a dream after someone has died. This symbolizes the person's soul and its transformation after he or she has died.

Buzzard

The buzzard is an unusual bird to dream about. Traditionally, the appearance of a buzzard can indicate good and bad luck, the birth of a baby, and the curing of an illness or disease. A buzzard flying over your home is a sure sign that visitors will be coming. However, it's a sign of misfortune if a buzzard flies over a church while a wedding is taking place.

Since buzzards clean up the landscape, dreaming of them can indicate a clearing out and cleansing period in your life. It indicates a time of re-evaluation. If a buzzard flies away as you approach it in your dream, it's a sign that a potential problem is being resolved. A group of buzzards in your dream is a sign that others are talking about you behind your back.

Camel

In the East, the camel is considered a lazy animal. Consequently, to dream of a camel is a sign that something needs to be done, but hard work and effort is required. However, as the camel is also a sign of endurance, the dreamer will find the necessary strength and energy to complete the task. Camels have the strength and energy to go for long periods without a drink, as they store water in their humps. In a dream this can indicate a quest that seems endless, but eventually ends in success. To dream of a number of camels is a sign of ultimate wealth gained through business dealings.

Canary

Canaries are native to Madeira, the Azores, and the Canary Islands. They were introduced into Europe in the early 1600s. People keep them as pets, because they are colorful and the male birds sing beautifully.

Dreaming of a canary is a sign that something unexpected will cause you great pleasure. If the canary is singing in your dream, it's a sign of happiness, love, and contentment.

Cat

The cat has been domesticated for more than four thousand years. The ancient Egyptians associated them with the goddesses Isis and Bastet, and worshipped them. Tens of thousands of cat mummies have been discovered, showing just how revered they were.[6] In Egypt it was a capital offense to kill a cat, even accidentally.

In the East, the cat is traditionally considered a sign of bad luck and danger. There are a number of reasons for this. It is believed that cats are able to see spirits in the dark. In parts of China, they are believed to get onto the roofs of houses and steal the moonbeams. In Taiwan it is believed that dead cats should not be buried, as they might turn into demons. If a cat jumps over a coffin, it is believed that the corpse will haunt the area.[7] Consequently, to dream of a cat is considered a warning of problems and hostility.

However, dreaming of a cat can also be a sign of longevity, as the Chinese words for "cat" and "octogenarian" are homophones. Consequently, to dream of a cat while you are ill is a sign that you'll recover and enjoy a long life.

Fortunately, cats usually fare better in dreams in the West, as they are considered a sign of good luck, playfulness, contentment, intuition, femininity, fertility, independence, and new beginnings. Some of these associations come from Bastet, the ancient Egyptian goddess of love, fertility, and the home. She had the head of a cat and the body of a woman.

Cats have also been associated with witches, and this probably dates back to the medieval superstition that Satan enjoyed shapeshifting himself into a black cat. In fact, this superstition may be much older, because in Greek legend a woman named Galenthias was turned into a cat and became a priestess of the Hecate cult.

The interpretation of a cat in a dream can be either positive or negative depending on how the dreamer feels about cats when he or she is awake. Someone who dislikes cats will see them as fearsome animals in dreams. The cat can symbolically reveal personal fears and weaknesses the person has. Conversely, someone who loves cats will see them as indicating positive aspects of his or her character. If the cat in your dream needs love and attention, it's a sign that you are not receiving everything you desire in your life. You should start paying more attention to your own needs.

Caterpillar

Caterpillars are considered lowly animals that are partway through their metamorphosis into adult moths or butterflies. Because of the different stages they go through before emerging as moths and butterflies, they are often considered symbols of reincarnation. Consequently, to dream of caterpillars is a sign that you are going through a stage of transformation and inner growth. This is often accompanied by feelings of isolation and despair that disappear only when you realize that this stage is an essential part of your growth and development.

Centaur

In Greek mythology, the centaur has the head, arms, and torso of a man, and the lower body and legs of a horse. In astrology, the centaur symbolizes the sign of Sagittarius. The centaur symbolizes the two sides of mankind's nature, and the conflict that occurs between them. In Christianity, the centaur symbolizes sensuality, and humanity's animal and spiritual nature.

Dreaming of a centaur is a sign that you have two conflicting points of view, and you need to think carefully before deciding which one to choose.

Centipede

During the day, centipedes can be found under bark, stones, and litter all around the world. At night, they come out and feed on other small invertebrate animals. They have from fourteen to 177 pairs of legs, which enable them to move quickly in pursuit of their prey.

Dreaming of centipedes is a sign that you will start something on a very small scale and gradually build it up into something worthwhile. Centipedes also exemplify persistence and show that once you've taken the first few steps, nothing will prevent you from succeeding.

Cerberus

In Greek and Roman mythology, Cerberus was a large three-headed dog that guarded the gates in front of Hades to prevent anyone who had crossed the River Styx from escaping. Cerberus usually has a mane made of serpents, as well as a serpent tail. The final labor of Heracles (frequently Romanized as *Hercules*) was to capture Cerberus alive. Heracles achieved this task with great difficulty, and brought Cerberus to his king.

Dreaming of Cerberus is a sign that you feel hemmed in or restricted in some way. You need to allow some time and space for you and your needs.

Cheetah

The ancient Egyptians revered the cheetah, and many tomb paintings include them. The heads of cheetahs were carved into the bed King Tutankhamun lay on in his tomb. The ancient Egyptians trained cheetahs to hunt antelope and rewarded them with butter every time they succeeded.

Cheetahs are renowned for their speed, and are considered the fastest of all land animals. They developed their speed because, unlike most large cats, they hunt during the daytime. Consequently, if you dream of a cheetah it's a sign that you'll need to act speedily and decisively to resolve a particular situation that is going on in your life. This can force you out of your comfort zone if you are naturally timid and unwilling to act unless forced to do so.

Chicken

The domestic chicken is found all around the world and plays a major role in human diets. Chickens are virtually flightless, and because of this, dreaming of a chicken is a sign that you are trapped on the ground and have temporarily lost contact with the spiritual and intuitive sides of your nature.

As chickens are also associated with cowardice, you might be trapped on the ground as you are fearful or worried about seizing a particular opportunity.

A hen with her chicks is a sign of domestic happiness. It can also be related to feelings from your early childhood.

See also ROOSTER.

Chimera

In Greek mythology, the chimera is a creature with the head, mane, and legs of a lion; the body of a goat; and the tail of a dragon. Homer was the first person to describe the chimera. Today, the word *chimera* is used to describe something that is fanciful, imaginative, or unreal.

If you dream of a chimera, it's a sign that you consider something illusory or fanciful to be real.

Chimpanzee

We share all but 1.5 percent of our genetic material with chimpanzees, and because chimpanzees are so much like us, people have always been fascinated by them. During the sixteenth century, Portuguese explorers called chimpanzees "Pygmies." The word *chimpanzee* was first used by Europeans in 1738. It is derived from the Bantu word *kivili-chimpense*, which means "mock man."

Chimpanzees use a wide variety of gestures to communicate with each other. They use tools, and learn quickly from observing others. Sadly, they are killed for food, which means their numbers are declining every year.

Dreaming of a chimpanzee is a sign that a playful, fun-loving side of your nature wants to express itself. This often occurs if you have been working hard for a long period of time, and is a sign that you are overdue for a vacation. If it's not possible to have a vacation in the near future, you need to spend relaxing times with friends and loved ones.

See also MONKEY.

Cicada

The ancient Greeks kept cicadas as pets. According to Plato, cicadas were originally men who were so devoted to music that they forgot to look after themselves and died, leaving only their music as proof that they had ever lived.

Cicadas remain underground for many years, using an unpredictable breeding cycle to confound their predators. Even though some 98 percent of them die while still underground, trillions of them still manage to emerge on the same evening. Their predators eat many of them, but because they can't eat them all, many survive to create the next generation.

Dreaming of a cicada is a sign that your time of "hibernation" is coming to an end. You need to make plans, and get ready to make a strong move forward.

See also INSECTS.

Cock

See ROOSTER.

Cockatrice

See BASILISK.

Cockroach

Cockroaches have survived as a species for more than three hundred million years and are one of the oldest fossil insects.[8] Although most people loathe cockroaches, they are considered protective spirits in parts of France and Russia. Their arrival is a sign of good luck. Naturally, it is also an indication of bad luck when they leave.[9]

Dreaming of a cockroach is a sign that you're starting to understand and accept feelings or emotions that you previously repressed. Unpleasant situations or experiences in the past might need to be re-examined dispassionately to see what lessons can be gained from them.

Cow

Cows have provided humans with milk, cheese, meat, and leather for thousands of years. Cows were venerated in ancient Egypt. Sacred cows were kept at the temple of the Greek goddess Hera at Argos. In India, cows are considered sacred as they provide nourishment. In Buddhism, there's a close relationship between the cow and people's gradual progress towards enlightenment.

In the Bible, Joseph recounts many of his dreams. He also interpreted many of Pharaoh's dreams, including one about seven fat cows and seven lean cows. Joseph interpreted these as seven years of plenty, followed by seven years of famine. The pharaoh acted on this interpretation and was able to build up food stores to ensure everyone was fed during the seven years of famine (Genesis 41:17–38).

In the West, cows symbolize motherhood, because they provide milk and food. Milking cows were valuable assets in the past. Cows are considered placid, passive animals. For this reason, to dream of one is a sign that you need to become more active and take control of your life. If a man dreams of a cow, it's a sign that he's making contact with the feminine side of his nature.

See also BULL and OX.

Coyote

Coyotes are found throughout North America. As predators, they help to control the environment by scavenging for food when they can't catch small animals. The coyote is a trickster in the Native American tradition. However, some tribes consider coyotes to be the embodiment of evil, and relate them to winter and death. The coyote is also related to sex, as the male coyote has a reputation as a satyr.

Dreaming of a coyote is a sign that you are not creating something because of concerns about what other people might think or say. It can also relate to concerns about one's sexuality.

Crab

The crab is the symbol of Cancer, the fourth sign of the Western zodiac. The Sun is in Cancer between June 22nd and July 22nd.

Because crabs carry their home around with them, dreaming about a crab is a sign that you possess the ability to create a home wherever you happen to be, and are likely to enjoy a rich home and family life. It also shows that you can work well within a team.

However, if a crab bites or pinches you, it is a sign that you are reluctant to accept change and find it hard to let go.

Crane

According to Roman tradition, the god Hermes invented writing after seeing the different shapes cranes make while dancing and flying. The crane has always been considered an emblem of longevity and wisdom. Because it flies high over the dirty and dusty world, it is considered pure, clean, and of blameless character. It is a good omen to dream of a crane, as this means that you will fly high in your career. To dream of two cranes flying together is even better, as this means that others are supporting you in your ambition to progress in your life and career.

It is not a good omen to dream of a crane flying away from you, as this portends the death of someone close to you.

Cricket

In China, the cricket symbolizes death and rebirth, since it lays its eggs in the ground and emerges as a fully grown insect after its larval stage. In China, as well as in many Mediterranean countries, it's a sign of good luck if a cricket makes its home inside your house.

Crickets represent joy and happiness. If you dream of a cricket, it's a sign that you're missing out on much of the joy and pleasure that life has to offer. It is an indication that you need to re-evaluate your life and seek more happiness in small things.

Crocodile
See ALLIGATOR.

Crow
The ancient Greeks associated the crow with monogamy. The Celts considered it a sacred bird, as their goddess Badb appeared in battle in the shape of a crow. In Native American folklore, both the crow and raven are tricksters who can change shape at will.

To dream of a crow is a sign that you need time on your own to sort out your feelings. It is a time of introspection, melancholy, and even sorrow, but you'll emerge from it stronger than ever before. In the past, the crow used to indicate anger and discord. Make sure you examine your feelings before speaking to others. Be kind.

Cuckoo
In Tibet, the cuckoo is considered a sacred animal. In the Sichuan province of China, people pay great attention to the cuckoo, as it enables them to choose the correct day to start different tasks on the farm. Consequently, to dream of a cuckoo is a sign that your timing is good and that you can move forward towards your goal. It also shows that you're adaptable and ready to make changes when necessary.

Since cuckoos lay their eggs in other birds' nests, dreaming of a cuckoo can be related to feelings of fidelity and faithfulness, as well as possible suspicions about your partner.

Deer

Deer are associated with gentleness, tenderness, and vulnerability. Consequently, to dream of a deer is a sign that your tenderness, compassion, and understanding will be required to help someone who needs protection. It can also be an indication that you're easily hurt and would benefit from some gentle nurturing and pampering.

People used to believe that deer shed tears. However, it is now known that what appear to be tears are actually oily secretions from tear pits. William Shakespeare mentioned the tears of a deer:

"A poor sequester'd stag,

That from the hunter's aim had ta'en a hurt,

Did come to languish . . . and the big round tears

Cours'd one another down his innocent nose

In piteous chase." (*As You Like It*, act 2, scene 1.)

The deer is the subject of many legends in China. The word deer (*lu*) is a homophone of a word that means "prosperity." Deer are also considered a sign of longevity, as their horns are one of the ingredients in an herbal medicine to promote longevity. Consequently, in China, to dream of a deer is a sign that you'll do well financially and enjoy a long life.

See also MOOSE and STAG.

Dinosaur

Dinosaurs were reptiles that lived some sixty-five million years ago, in the Mesozoic era. They seldom appear in dreams. When they do, they usually relate to basic, instinctive urges, such as survival and reproduction of the species. Dinosaurs symbolize memories and feelings from early childhood that are having an effect on your current life. They can also indicate letting go of something from your past that has been holding you back. It's a sign of increased confidence and faster progress in the future.

Dog

Dogs evolved from wolves, and were first domesticated some twelve to fourteen thousand years ago. The ancient Egyptians believed dogs acted as guides and messengers in the underworld. They could also take messages from the living to the dead. The Greeks had a two- or three-headed dog named Cerberus who guarded the entrance to Hades. He would not allow living people in, and also refused to let dead people out.

As with cats, your own feelings about dogs will have a major effect on the interpretation of them in your dreams. If you like dogs, your dreams that include them will relate to friendship, devotion, loyalty, and faithfulness. If the dog is licking you, it's a sign that old emotional wounds are being healed. If the dog is barking with excitement, it's a sign that you are welcomed and accepted by others. However, if the dog is barking because it's angry, it's a sign of problems ahead. It is an indication of problems between friends or family members if you dream of two dogs fighting. A large dog is a sign of protection. However, a small dog suggests a lack of confidence. If you dream about your own dog, it's a symbol of the positive qualities you possess. Dreaming of a puppy, or puppies, is always a positive sign and symbolizes energy, enthusiasm, and youthfulness. It can relate to your feelings about your own children.

For many people, dreaming of a dog is a sign of love and devotion. These people often had unhappy childhoods, and may feel that the only love they experienced at that time came from the family dog.

Dreaming of a black dog can be a sign of sadness, depression, and loneliness.

If you don't like dogs, any dogs you see in your dreams are likely to be aggressive. This is a sign that someone at work is making your life difficult, most probably because of envy.

The dog is the eleventh animal in the Chinese zodiac. Traditionally, if a dog bit you in your dream, it was an indication that your dead ancestors were hungry, and you had to send them offerings of food and money. To dream of a dog running towards you is a good omen, as it means that you will ultimately be wealthy. To dream of a sleeping dog is a sign of faithfulness and protection. It denotes a strong, stable relationship.

However, it is not a good omen to dream of a dog that is snarling or aggressive. This is a sign of family arguments and difficulties.

Dolphin

Dolphins are considered intelligent, graceful, and playful animals. If you dream of dolphins, these associations will play an important role in what is going on in your life. It usually means that you're being extended and challenged mentally, and are benefiting from this stimulation. It's also a sign that you need to set aside time for play.

Dolphins also relate to communication and can indicate that your subconscious mind has important information that it's trying to transmit to your conscious mind. If the dolphins are leaping in your dream, it's a sign of contentment and happiness. It shows that all aspects of your life are going well.

Donkey

Today, the donkey is often considered a symbol of stupidity. However, a donkey was present at the Nativity and also carried Jesus into Jerusalem on Palm Sunday. This fulfilled a prophecy, and also demonstrated meekness. Consequently, in the Christian tradition, the donkey signifies patience and humility. To this day, the donkey has a dark stripe running down its back, crossed by another stripe at its shoulders. Jesus is said to have given the cross to the donkey after His triumphant entry into Jerusalem.

In ancient Egypt, donkeys were used as beasts of burden. They helped the Egyptians expand their trading empire, as donkeys uncomplainingly carry 30 percent of their body weight.

In ancient China, a white donkey was the steed of the Immortals. In India, the donkey is also the steed of gods, but it is a negative symbol, as these are the gods of death.

There are two main interpretations if you dream about a donkey. The first shows that you need to become more patient, accepting, and nonjudgmental. The second interpretation shows that you are indulging in sexual fantasies that have no relationship to what you would do in real life. It is also an indication that the sexual side of your life needs more attention. It's a sign of leadership ability, persistence, and determination if you're leading the donkey by a rope. If the donkey is braying, it's a sign that a family disagreement is being resolved. If you're riding the donkey, it's a sign of humility. If someone else is riding the donkey, you may feel that you're doing far more than your share of the work. If the donkey is carrying a heavy load, it's a sign of travel to new and interesting places. It's a sign of bad luck if you fall off a donkey or if a donkey kicks you.

Dove

In ancient Greece, the dove was sacred to Aphrodite. In Islam, the dove is also a sacred bird, as it protected Mohammed during his flight from Mecca. In most cultures, a dove symbolizes peace, innocence, love, reconciliation, fulfilment, and spirituality. This is probably because Noah sent out three doves after the Flood. One returned with an olive branch, which was considered a sign of reconciliation with God. A white dove also traditionally symbolizes the Holy Spirit. Doves also symbolize the soul, and in medieval art, doves are sometimes shown emerging from the mouths of dead saints.

If a dove appears in your dream, it's a sign that you possess a creative potential that you have not yet developed. You'll find numerous opportunities to grow and develop creatively. As you develop creatively, you'll gain contentment and peace of mind. A dove also indicates a happy home and family life.

Dragon

The dragon is a mythological animal that looks something like a winged, fire-belching crocodile. The dragon is the fifth sign in the Chinese zodiac. It represents the east direction, sunrise, and rain. In the East, the dragon is considered to be good-natured, supportive, and caring.

In the West, dragons have been regarded as evil, vicious kidnappers of innocent young maidens. In the Middle Ages, the dragon was considered synonymous with sin. This is because of two references in the Bible: "Thou shalt tread upon the lion and adder: the young lion and the dragon shalt thou trample under feet" (Psalm 91:13), and "And the great dragon was cast out, that old serpent, called the Devil, and Satan, which deceiveth the whole world." (Revelation 12:9).

However, the ancient Britons used the dragon as a national symbol on their standards when they went to war, and a red dragon is still a prominent feature on the flag of Wales.

To dream of a dragon is a sign of strength, potency, and vigor. Consequently, it is an indication of fertility. The dragon is also a magical animal. For this reason, to dream of a dragon is also a sign that you have more abilities and talents than you think you do. In the past, dreaming of a dragon was a sign that the dreamer would meet the emperor. Generally speaking, to dream of a dragon is an omen of good luck.

See also KOMODO DRAGON.

Duck

Ducks are found all around the world. Small children enjoy feeding them, and many adults enjoy hunting them for sport or food. Although the word *duck* is considered genderless, it actually refers to the female of the species. The correct name for the male is *drake*. Because ducks are at home on water, land, and in the air, they symbolize the possibility of transformation. Consequently, to dream of a duck is a sign that you should be ready and willing to change, as this will open up a variety of opportunities for you.

The early Christians depicted ducks on the portals of churches. This was because ducks constantly chatter, and the church fathers wanted people who talked incessantly to stay away. Consequently, to dream of several chattering ducks is a sign that you should not indulge in mindless chatter and gossip.

The duck has an interesting reputation in China. In eastern China, for instance, the word for "duck" is a homophone for the word for "homosexual." In northern China, the word for "penis" is a homophone for "duck." This is an instance in which similar-sounding words have created a negative impression, and over the years the duck has suffered as a result. However, to dream a pair of ducks is a sign of love and romance, and to dream of a mandarin duck is a sign of a happy marriage.

Eagle

Ever since antiquity, the eagle has been considered the king of birds, and was used as a symbol by kings and other leaders. An eagle was the companion of Zeus. In Roman art an eagle carried the soul of deceased rulers to the gods after his cremation. Roman legions also used the eagle as a symbol of strength on their banners. When an emperor died, an eagle was released from the funeral pyre, symbolizing the soul heading upwards to the gods.

Consequently, it's not surprising that the eagle symbolizes strength and courage in dream interpretation. To dream of an eagle is a sign that you will have the necessary strength to achieve your desires, even though you may feel isolated and on your own most of the time. It also shows that you'll pay attention to all the details and will make good decisions.

Dreaming of an eagle also shows you have leadership potential. If you dream of an eagle soaring high into the air, it's a sign that you're seeking spiritual growth. Dreaming of a bald eagle is a sign of patriotism for people in the USA.

Echidna

The echidna is a stocky, spiny anteater with a short tail. It is native to Australia and New Guinea. When disturbed by its enemies, it curls up into a ball like a hedgehog, wedges itself tightly into a crevice, or digs downwards into the earth until only its spines are visible. They are shy, slow-moving animals that can live up to fifty years. To dream of an echidna is a sign that you should cease holding yourself back, and stand up for yourself when necessary.

Echidna was also a mythical creature that was half woman, half serpent. She lived in a deep cave and was called "the mother of all monsters." She gave birth to many other Grecian mythical creatures, including the chimera and the sphinx.

If you dream of echidnas, you are seeking someone or something that can't be found. It is time to let it go and move on with your life.

See also CHIMERA and SPHINX.

Eel

Eels are smooth-skinned, snakelike, predatory fish. In many parts of the world, but especially in China, the phallic shape of the eel is related to sexuality.[10] Because eels live in water, which symbolizes the subconscious mind, dreaming of an eel shows that powerful, hidden sexual impulses are near the surface of your mind. Frequently, these express them-selves as anxiety and lack of confidence, especially con-cerning sexual matters. It's a sign of good luck ahead if you manage to catch and hold on to an eel in your dream.

Elephant

The elephant is the largest terrestrial mammal, and symbol-izes strength, power, intelligence, and longevity. In Asia, the elephant is considered a powerful, wise, and happy animal.

The Indian god Indra rides an elephant; and Ganesh, son of the great god Shiva, has the head of an elephant. In Africa, the elephant symbolizes strength, longevity, and happiness. In China, elephants symbolize strength and intelligence. As well as being highly intelligent, elephants are famed for their memories. According to Aristotle, the male elephant abstained from sex during the two-year gestation period of his mate. In fact, this is not the case. However, because of this belief, elephants are considered to be careful, chaste, and prudent.

Nowadays, the elephant is considered an intelligent, moral, and faithful animal. Naturally, it also symbolizes strength, ambition, motivation, power, and the ability to carry on indefinitely. To dream of an elephant indicates all of these qualities are present in your life, and should be harnessed and utilized. An elephant can symbolize all the qualities you should be making use of in your everyday life.

Elephants are renowned for their memory. They may appear in your dreams if you're concerned that you may not remember something important. Several people have told me that they experienced dreams about elephants while studying for important exams. Elephants have large brains and are extremely intelligent. Interestingly, elephants, dolphins, and some primates are the only animals that can recognize themselves in a mirror.

If you see yourself riding an elephant in your dream, it means that your desires will be realized and fulfilled. You will ultimately find yourself in a position of responsibility and prestige.

It is rare to have a negative dream about an elephant. It's a sign of repression and frustration to dream of elephants attacking or fighting each other. If you are running away from an elephant, it's a sign that you're afraid to use your personal power and strength.

Dreaming of an elephant's tusks is not auspicious, as it can be a sign of an early death. In other words, you will not live long enough to enjoy a peaceful and happy retirement.

Falcon

In ancient Egypt, the falcon was considered sacred to the sun god Ra. Horus, along with other gods, was able to assume the form of a falcon, or a human with a falcon's head, when necessary. Falcons have been tamed and trained for sporting purposes for at least 2,500 years. Falconry is still practiced today, but was most popular in the Middle Ages when younger members of the royal families of Europe participated in the sport.

To dream of a falcon is a sign that your innate spirituality can, and should, be tamed and become a part of every aspect of your life.

Ferret

The ferret is a small, inquisitive, weasel-like animal that has somehow gained an unwarranted reputation for deceitfulness and dishonesty. Dreaming of a ferret is a sign that someone close to you is not to be trusted, and is undermining you in some way.

Firefly

Fireflies, or lightning bugs, are winged insects that produce light in their abdomens. Dreaming of fireflies is a positive sign, as it shows you have the ability to get on well with others and will always find light in the darkness.

Fish

In the West, fish are believed to provide insights into the working of the subconscious mind. This is because they live in water, a powerful symbol of the subconscious. Fish can also symbolize fertility, life, emotions, and the Divine. The connection with God is likely to be because the fish is one of the oldest symbols of Jesus Christ, and this possibly came about because Christians were baptized in water. Another possibility is that the first letters of the Greek words for "Jesus Christ, Son of God, Savior" (*Iesous Christos Theou Huios Soter*) spell *Icthius*, which is Greek for "fish."

Jesus said to Simon and Andrew, "Follow me, and I will make you fishers of men" (Matthew 4:19). Yet another possibility is that it became a symbol after Jesus used five barley loaves and two small fish to feed the crowd of five thousand (Matthew 14:17, Mark 6:38, Luke 9:13, and John 6:9).

In most people's dreams, fish tend to be beautiful and colorful. However, there is no need for concern if the fish in your dreams are dull, unattractive, or swimming in dirty water. This is a sign that you need to nurture yourself, and take one day at a time until matters in your life improve.

The fish is also related to Pisces, the twelfth sign of the zodiac. The Sun passes through Pisces between February

18th and March 20th. Consequently, someone who is interested in astrology may see someone of this sign as a fish in his or her dream.

In the East, fish symbolize wealth and abundance. The Chinese words for "fish" and "affluence" are homophones. For this reason, to dream of fish is a sign of future prosperity. To dream of two fish swimming in the water is an indication of a highly compatible sexual relationship, as well as happiness and harmony.

Carl Jung believed that fish symbolized a deep level of our subconscious minds. Consequently, fish indicate deeply hidden fears, concerns, hopes, and wishes that have not yet filtered up into the conscious mind.

It is a sign of fertility and good relationships if you dream of many fish in your dream. If the fish are swimming in clear water, it's an indication that your finances are about to improve.

It's an indication that you're uncovering repressed emotions if you dream that you're fishing. Eating a fish is a sign that you feel happy and satisfied with your progress in life.

It's a sign of a busy future social life if a wide variety of different fish appear in the same dream.

Frederick Greenwood (1830–1909), a well-known Victorian journalist, recounted a recurring dream he had involving fish in his book *Imagination in Dreams*:

"I dream that I am walking in the fields. I saunter along idly, pleasantly, through level meadows, and by and by come to a narrow stream; the whole scene being just such a one as the angler resorts to in Hampshire. But I am no fisherman, and never think of rod-fishing except as a dull delight about which a vast amount of lyrical nonsense is sung to one old tune. Yet, when I look into the stream, and see there many good fish gliding, I wish for a rod and a creel. The wish is no sooner formed than it rises to eagerness, for at every moment the fish become larger and larger and still more plentiful. Before long they might be baled out with a bucket; yet a little while and they might be cast to the banks with a malt-shovel. Rapidly changing in shape and size from pretty one-pound trout to great-eyed, loose-mouthed, cod-like monsters, they presently fill the whole bed of the stream—fill it pile-high in a horrible sweltering heap; which becomes more horrible still in another moment, when the ghastly creatures die and fall to pieces. An unendurable sight, instantly followed by the relief of waking, but not to shake off the squalid terror of the scene for hours after. At intervals of months, or more frequently of years, this dream has been repeated many times, with no difference of detail whatever."[11]

See also DOLPHIN, EEL, MERMAID, OCTOPUS, SALMON, SHARK, and WHALE.

Flamingo

Flamingos are wading birds that often stand on one leg, with the other leg tucked under their bodies.

Dreaming of a flamingo is a sign that you're seeking balance and equilibrium in your life. Dreaming of a pink flamingo shows that your soul is developing and progressing in this incarnation.

Fly

The common housefly has always been connected with filth, decay, and death. Consequently, in the past it was considered an omen that if a person dreamt of a fly he or she would die soon. Beelzebub, a devil mentioned in the Bible, was often depicted as a fly. Flies spread cholera, dysentery, tuberculosis, typhoid, and many other illnesses by excreting, vomiting, and walking over food. On the positive side, they help recycle dead and decaying matter.

Flies usually have negative connotations in dreams today. If you dream of a fly, it's a sign that other people are trying to influence you, and may even try to use emotional blackmail. Alternatively, you may be surrounded by negative people. Dreaming of a solitary fly gives you the ability to move quickly to resolve a problem. Dreaming of many flies is a sign that you're too busy with everyday concerns to make plans for the future.

In the East, the seemingly mindless flitting of a fly symbolizes a wandering, restless soul.

Fox

All around the world, the fox is considered a sly and cunning animal. Chinese folktales say that when a fox reached the age of fifty, it was able to turn itself into a woman. At the age of one hundred, it could turn into a young girl, and at the age of one thousand it would become a celestial fox. People believed that evil spirits rode on the backs of foxes. In China, dreaming of a fox is not a good sign, as it indicates potential venereal disease. Native American myths portray the fox as a trickster, and someone who can change shape at will.

In the West, it's considered a sign of danger to dream of a fox. This could be a sign that others see you as sly and cunning, and you need to be more open and honest.

However, there are positive interpretations, too. Foxes are shrewd, intelligent, and cautious animals, with excellent survival skills. Foxes can be a sign that you should be cautious, and act only when you are convinced it is the right time to make a move. If you chase or catch a fox in your dream, it's a sign that you'll be ten steps ahead of your enemies and anyone else who does not wish you well. It's a sign of an enjoyable social event if you dream you are one of a group of riders out fox hunting.

Frog

In ancient Mesopotamia, the frog symbolized fertility. In ancient Egypt, frogs symbolized reincarnation. The early Christian church associated frogs with the devil.

In Korea, it is believed that to dream of a frog indicates the birth of a son. In Japan, dreaming of a frog is a sign that good luck is coming.

In dreams, frogs almost always have sexual connotations and show that the dreamer needs to overcome his or her negative attitudes towards sex and start living life with feelings of joy and liberation.

Frogs also represent transformation, and show that you're letting certain aspects of the past go and are starting to look forward again.

Furies

In Roman mythology, the three Furies were mythical winged creatures with snakes for hair. (In Greek mythology, they were known as the Eumenides.) They were called daughters of Gaia (the Earth), and were said to have appeared fully formed from the blood of Uranus. Consequently, blood dripped from their eyes. They were also known as Daughters of the Night and Daughters of Darkness. Their names were Tisiphone (the Avenger of Blood), Alecto (the Implacable), and Megaera (the Jealous). The Furies sought vengeance for all crimes that went unpunished, or were ethically, rather than criminally, wrong. Their power was so strong that they were able to continue punishing people long after they had died.

If you dream of the Furies, it's a sign that you need to right something that is wrong. You'll need courage and persistence to do this, and may not receive much help from other people.

Gargoyle

Traditionally, gargoyles protect buildings from evil spirits. In dreams, they are sometimes seen as winged animals with talons, a tail, and a demonic face. They have the ability to turn themselves into stone whenever they wish.

Dreaming of a gargoyle is a sign that you're protected from the envy, gossip, and malice of others.

Giraffe

Some giraffes reach nineteen feet in height, making them the tallest animals in the world. This height plays an important part in dream interpretation. If you dream of a giraffe, you may be wanting to look at a particular situation from a different point of view. You might want to rise above petty squabbles and disagreements with others. You might even want to see what's over the horizon. Alternatively, you might be looking upwards and searching for a spiritual dimension in your life.

Goat

Goats are intriguing animals. They are intelligent, inquisitive, mischievous, and frequently aggressive. They have distinct personalities, enjoy human contact, and are loyal and friendly. However, in folklore, they are considered lustful, lecherous, foul smelling, and treacherous. In mythology, goats fare even worse, as they were thought to have been created by the devil and were therefore considered demonic. In stark contrast to this is Pan, the goat-god who is impish, kind, gentle, and friendly.

In Greek mythology, a goat nurtured Zeus when he was a young child. In Christianity, a lascivious goat symbolized Satan. In the Bible, Jesus tells a parable about a shepherd who separated his sheep from the goats, placing the sheep on the right and the goats on the left. After promising the sheep on the right great rewards in heaven, Jesus continues with: "Then shall he say also unto them on the left hand [the goats], Depart from me, ye cursed, into everlasting fire, prepared for the devil and his angels" (Matthew 25:41). The goat is also the animal that symbolizes Capricorn, and a slow, steady, serious approach to life.

As a result of these conflicting ideas about goats, it's not always easy to explain the meaning of a goat in a dream. It can indicate that you're denying your innate sexual nature. However, dreaming of a male goat can indicate virility, and a female goat fertility. Sometimes it indicates that you're contemplating something foolish or mischievous. Conversely, it can also indicate that you're being overly serious. Dreaming of a mountain goat is a clear sign that you should start moving ahead with new projects. If the goat in your dream is butting you, it's a sign that someone is trying to butt into your life.

Goose

When I lived in London, I was fortunate enough to live beside the River Thames. Most mornings, I had to pass a highly aggressive goose while walking to the railway station. I occasionally missed my train, as the goose would not let me or the other commuters get past him. Consequently, I consider geese to be nasty, vicious birds. However, I still think geese look majestically serene on water and beautiful in flight.

According to Roman tradition, a flock of geese saved the capital city by alerting guards to an attack from a Gaulish army in 387 BCE. After that, sacred geese were kept in Rome. They were sacred to Juno and considered a symbol of love, fertility, and happy marriage, as well as vigilance.

Partly because of this Roman tradition, the goose is still considered a symbol of a happy marriage. However, the main reason for this interpretation is that the goose has just one partner in its life. Pictures of two flying geese make popular wedding gifts as they symbolize a long and happy marriage. To dream of geese is a sign of a long and happy union.

Grasshopper

In China, it is considered good luck if a grasshopper spends time in your home. (See also CRICKET.)

Grasshoppers are able to leap almost twenty times the length of their bodies. Children think grasshoppers are playing when they do this, and thus the grasshopper has become a symbol of joy. If you dream of a grasshopper, it's a sign that you're lacking joy in your life. If you dream of a swarm of grasshoppers, it's a sign that you're holding yourself back by being overly rigid and unforgiving.

Gryphon

The gryphon, griffon, or griffin is a mythical animal that has the legs and head of an eagle, and the body of a lion. Its claws are those of an eagle. Female gryphons have the wings of an eagle, but male gryphons, which are depicted rarely, usually lack wings. The eagle is considered the king of birds, and the lion the king of beasts, making gryphons a particularly powerful symbol. Gryphons were sacred to the sun and had the task of protecting hidden treasures. The gryphon lives in the elements of Air and Fire, as the eagle corresponds to Air, and the lion, Fire. The gryphon symbolizes courage, strength, generosity, eternal vigilance, and divine power.

In China, the gryphon is a symbol of enlightenment and wisdom. In Christianity, the gryphon was considered a symbol of Jesus, who was both human and divine.

Dreaming of a gryphon is a sign that you can accomplish much more than you are currently doing. It shows that you should set your sights higher than ever before, make a plan, and then work hard to achieve your new, higher goals.

Hare

The hare symbolizes the moon, as it sleeps during the day and is active at night. It is also closely related to mother Earth, as it's highly fertile. Because of its voracious sexual appetite, the hare was considered the favorite animal of Aphrodite, the Greek goddess of love. In medieval Europe, people thought that hares, as well as cats, were witches' familiars. People believed that witches could turn themselves into hares whenever they wished to harm others. Consequently, it was considered bad luck if a hare crossed your path. The custom of carrying a "lucky" rabbit's foot began at this time, as people believed they would avert witches' spells.[12]

The hare, or rabbit, is the fourth animal in the Chinese zodiac. Because the rabbit breeds so prolifically, the rabbit symbolizes fertility, sexuality, and rapid increase.

To dream of rabbits or hares is a sign that whatever is important to you will progress rapidly in the near future. You'll be able to avert potential danger and remain focused on your goal. Rabbits and hares are also a sign that you need to make more use of your intuition, as well as your imagination and creativity. If you catch a hare or rabbit in your dream, you'll win something of value. Conversely, if a hare or rabbit escapes from you, you'll lose something of value. Dreaming of a pet rabbit is a sign that you want to be appreciated, cared for, and loved.

Hawk

Amun Ra, the Egyptian creator god, listed the hawk as one of his most valuable possessions. In ancient Greece, the hawk was Apollo's messenger. The hawk symbolizes speed, energy, intuition, and aggression. During the Middle Ages, Christian artists used the hawk as a symbol of death.

To dream of a hawk is a sign that you need to be more proactive, decisive, and assertive in your life. It is a time for action. You also need to consider your life from a long-term point of view. If you do this, previously insurmountable obstacles will seem petty and insignificant.

Hedgehog

In China, the humble hedgehog has been associated with the overthrowing of an empire ever since Emperor Wu Cheng dreamt of large hedgehogs attacking his home. The next day, he ordered his men to kill every hedgehog in the city. In time, Wu Cheng lost his popularity and the people called him a hedgehog. Ever since then, in China, the poor hedgehog has been considered a predictor of destruction. However, in Japan and parts of China, the hedgehog is said to symbolize wealth.

During the Middle Ages, people in Europe considered the hedgehog a symbol of Satan.

To dream of a hedgehog is a sign that you need to face a difficult situation openly. You can't be defensive (prickly) or try to deny the problem exists (curling yourself up into a ball). The problem will take time to resolve, but the outcome will be positive for you.

See also PORCUPINE.

Hippogriff

The hippogriff is a mythical creature that is half gryphon and half horse. It has the head of an eagle and the body of a horse. Its wings are covered with feathers, and its claws are those of an eagle. The hippogriff symbolizes love, and anything that is impossible.

Dreaming of a hippogriff is a sign that you're about to fall in love with someone you had either not noticed or had overlooked before. Your love will be reciprocated, and the relationship will steadily grow and develop.

Hippopotamus

The hippopotamus is a huge and powerful animal that can weigh up to 7,000 pounds. In ancient Egypt, the male hippopotamus was considered a symbol of brutality and evil, because of his enormous appetite. However, the Egyptians also had a pregnant hippopotamus goddess, named Taueret, who looked after fertility, childbirth, women, and young children.

Because the hippopotamus is a gregarious animal, dreaming of one can be a sign of stimulating and rewarding social activity, as well as creativity. The hippopotamus is an immensely powerful animal that usually manages to get its own way. Consequently, dreaming of a hippopotamus can be a sign that you'll achieve your own goals without too much opposition from others.

If the hippo in your dreams is angry or aggressive, it's a sign that someone close to you is worried, upset, or concerned about something. You should offer your support and help.

If the hippo in your dream appears to be listless and unhappy, you may be concerned about your weight. However, this can also be a sign that something you're involved in is taking longer than you'd like to accomplish.

Horse

Horses are associated with freedom, speed, power, and achievement. Horses have played an important role in most cultures and even appear in Paleolithic cave paintings, showing how valuable they have been throughout history. According to Greek mythology, the god Poseidon created the first horse. The horse is used in Christian art to symbolize courage, stamina, and generosity.

It is usually a positive sign to dream of a horse, as it indicates peace and contentment. Mounting or racing a horse indicates an improvement in status or fortune. However, a horse that appears angry, or is trying to buck you off, is a sign of tension and disagreement. Unless you resolve the situation, your plans will not come into fruition. It's a sign that you are restricted in some way if the horse is injured, shackled, or confined. If you dream of a stallion, it is a sign of untapped sexual energy.

It has always been considered auspicious to dream of a white horse. This indicates fertility, happiness, success, and wealth. It is not uncommon for pregnant women to dream of a white horse.

Dreaming of a black horse is a sign of unwanted changes and fear of the unknown. It can also indicate unwanted attention from someone you don't care for.

If you're grooming a horse in your dream, it's a sign that you're gaining satisfaction from caring for others. This usually means you're providing their basic needs, such as food and shelter, but are also supplying love and support.

Dreaming of a flying horse with wings is a sign that you're not held back by the comments or restraints of others. You can soar as high as you wish.

The horse is the seventh animal in the Chinese zodiac. In ancient China there was a cult that worshipped ancestral horses. To dream of a wild horse or horses signifies that powerful instinctive energies are threatening to loose themselves from the subconscious mind. These energies are uncontrollable and can create turmoil as the dreamer tries to repress them. It is considered a desire for promotion in your career if you dream of a man leading a horse carrying precious objects.

Dreams that included horses are considered good omens, and relate to travel, visitors, and news. However, if the horses are in their stables it means that travel, visitors, or news are delayed.

In Artemidorus' *The Interpretation of Dreams* (c. 150 CE), there is a description of a dream involving a horse. A man dreamt that a friend of his had sent him a horse. Unbeknownst to the friend, the man was having an affair with his wife. In the dream a groom led the horse up two flights of stairs and into the bedchamber where the man was sleeping. Shortly after this, the man lost all contact with his mistress.

Artemidorus explained that the horse represented the mistress. As it was impossible for a horse to be on the third floor, the relationship between the man and his mistress could not continue.[13]

Hummingbird

Hummingbirds are tiny birds that can hover in the air and even fly backwards. Their wings can beat up to ninety times per second, and the humming sound they produce provided their name. Hummingbirds can fly up to thirty miles per hour.

Dreaming of a hummingbird is a sign of joy, happiness, and positivity. It also indicates recuperation from illness, and a happy and contented home and family life.

Hydra

The hydra is a creature from Greek mythology. It is a water snake with nine heads. (Some accounts say the hydra has as many as one hundred heads.) The hydra's breath was so poisonous that it killed anyone who came close. It was a difficult creature to kill—as each time a head was cut off, two more grew to replace it. The second labor of Hercules was to kill the Lernaean hydra that lived in a swamp near Lake Lerna. He succeeded in this task with the help of his charioteer who cauterized each wound as soon as Hercules cut off a head.

Dreaming of a hydra is a sign that you're facing an apparently insurmountable problem, and the more you examine the situation, the more complicated it becomes. You should examine the problem carefully and gradually resolve it by working at small parts of it at a time.

Hyena

The hyena was venerated by the ancient Egyptians, who believed a precious stone called the *hyaenia* could be found in its eyes. In Africa, the hyena has two opposing symbolic meanings. Because it is furtive and lives on carrion, it symbolizes cowardice. However, because it possesses powerful jaws, excellent eyesight, and a remarkable sense of smell, it also symbolizes knowledge and strength. Many people believe that because it eats the bones of dead animals, its stomach is full of lost souls, and consequently its howl is demonic.

If you dream of a hyena, it's a sign of emotional problems that need to be dealt with carefully. It can also be a sign that you are being preyed upon by others.

Ibis

The ibis is a long-legged wading bird, with a white body and a black head and tail, that was venerated in ancient Egypt. It was associated with the god Thoth, who was frequently depicted as a man with the head of an ibis.

Dreaming of an ibis is a sign of learning, wisdom, and enlightenment. It indicates an interest in the ancient teachings, and shows that you are developing spiritually.

Insects

Many people dream of bugs and insects that are often hard to identify. Insects demonstrate that small animals working together can achieve big results. Dreaming of insects is therefore a sign that you should pay attention to the small things in your life, and work well with others.

See also ANT, BEE, BEETLE, BUTTERFLY, CATERPILLAR, CENTIPEDE, CICADA, COCKROACH, CRICKET, FIREFLY, FLY, GRASSHOPPER, LOCUST, SCORPION, and SPIDER.

Jackal

The Egyptian god Anubis has the head of a jackal. Anubis weighs the souls of the dead to determine how good or evil they were. Because jackals are scavengers, people used to think they searched graveyards looking for corpses to feed on. The jackal is considered evil in both Hinduism and Buddhism. In Africa, the jackal symbolizes cowardice, and many people won't eat the heart of a jackal, fearing they may become cowardly themselves if they do.

To dream of a jackal is a sign that you need to deal with unhappy memories and unresolved issues from the past.

Jaguar

The jaguar is one of only two large cats in the Americas. Jaguars are solitary animals that are rarely seen. The Mayans and Aztecs associated the jaguar with fertility, the moon, sorcery, and Mother Earth. The jaguar is also associated with the shaman, and they are said to be able to exchange shapes and even souls.

Dreaming of a jaguar is a sign that you possess the necessary ability, power, assertiveness, and experience to tackle a significant project that you have been putting off.

Kangaroo

The kangaroo is famous for its ability to cover huge distances by leaping on its hind legs. Consequently, to dream of a kangaroo is a sign that you need to make a "leap of faith," if you are to progress in a particular endeavor. You should use the strength, speed, and agility of the kangaroo to achieve your immediate goals.

Kelpie

In the Celtic tradition, a kelpie, or kelpy, is a secretive water horse that haunts lochs, rivers, and streams in Scotland and Ireland. It is usually black but can also be white. Its skin is similar to that of a seal, and its mane is always dripping wet. It usually appears as a beautiful pony, but can metamorphose into a beautiful young girl to tempt young men into a fatal trap. It also tempts young children to ride on its back, and then drowns and eats them. Despite this, kelpies were also said to help millers grind their wheat by keeping the mill wheel working throughout the night.

Dreaming of a kelpie is a sign that you'll be offered something tempting, but should avoid it at all costs, as it will turn out to be a costly mistake.

Kingfisher

Because the brightly colored birds known as kingfishers often fly in pairs, they are a symbol of marital bliss, especially in China. "Kingfisher contact" is the term given to one of the thirty positions used in Chinese lovemaking. Consequently, to see a kingfisher in your dreams is a sign of sexual satisfaction and enjoyment.

In medieval times, people believed the kingfisher molted all its feathers. Consequently, it became a symbol of resurrection.

Kiwi

The kiwi is a flightless, almost blind bird that is native to New Zealand. Kiwis are nocturnal and use their strong sense of smell to locate insects and worms underground. Kiwis are monogamous, and it is usually the male kiwi that sits on the egg.

Dreaming of a kiwi is a sign that you're developing previously latent talents and have the potential to take these new skills a long way.

Koala

The koala is a herbivorous marsupial native to Australia. Koalas live almost entirely on the leaves of the eucalyptus tree. As 50 percent of these leaves consist of water, koalas hardly ever need to drink. In fact, the name *koala* means "no water" in the Dharuk language. The Dharuks were Aboriginal people who used to live in the area of present-day Sydney. *Dingo*, *wallaby*, and *wombat* are also Dharuk words. Koalas are slow-moving animals, with a low metabolic rate. They sleep up to eighteen hours each day.

Dreaming of a koala is a sign that you need to slow down and be more patient. Frantic activity often produces fewer results than does slow, steady progress.

Komodo Dragon

The komodo dragon is native to Indonesia and is the world's largest living lizard. It can grow to ten feet in length and often weighs around 150 pounds. The largest known komodo dragon weighed 370 pounds. In the absence of a male, the female monitor lizard can produce offspring by parthenogenesis, which means "virgin birth" in Greek. The komodo dragon was unknown in the West until 1910. In 1926, an adventurer named William Douglas Burden organized an expedition to capture one. He brought two live specimens back to the United States, but they soon died. His expedition inspired Burden's friend, Merian C. Cooper (1893–1973), a Hollywood producer and director, to make his movie *King Kong* in 1933.

Komodo dragons are often called "living dinosaurs," even though they are not directly related to dinosaurs. Dreaming of a komodo dragon is a sign that you've been in one place for too long and need to change your attitude, job, or home to avoid being considered a dinosaur yourself.

See also DRAGON and LIZARD.

Lamb

See SHEEP.

Leopard

The leopard is a solitary, predatory animal found in eastern and central Africa, as well as parts of southern Asia. In China, the leopard was associated with the moon, but in Africa it was related to the sun. In ancient Greece, it was associated with Dionysius, who was often depicted riding a leopard.

The leopard was sometimes referred to as the "great watcher," because the spots on its coat looked like eyes.

To dream of a leopard is a sign that hidden aspects of your nature—especially sensual, erotic, and violent elements—need to be handled carefully in order to avoid confrontations with others. If you dream of a leopard at the same time as dissension is going on in your life, it's a sign that you will overcome your opponents with ease. Dreaming of a leopard in a cage is a sign that an enemy is powerless to hurt you. If a leopard attacks you in your dream, it's a sign of obstacles on the path towards your ultimate goal.

The English author Anna Kavan (1901–68) wrote a short story called "A Visit," which describes how in a dream a leopard visited her one night and lay down in bed beside her. She enjoyed watching the rhythmic expansion and contraction of its chest, and savored "his natural odor, a wild primeval smell of sunshine, freedom, moon, and crushed leaves, combined with the cool freshness of the spotted hide, still damp with the midnight moisture of jungle plants." When she woke up in the morning, the leopard had left.[14]

Leviathan

The leviathan is a huge mythical sea monster that is mentioned in the Bible (Job 41:1–34, Psalms 74:14, Psalms 104:26, Isaiah 27:1, and Lamentations 4:3). It is described as serpent-like, with glowing, piercing eyes, and a scaly skin. It is able to crush ships and enjoys eating people who are rash enough to swim in the sea.

Dreaming of a leviathan is a sign that something you thought would be horrendous will not be nearly as difficult to handle as you thought. You may have to compromise or make adjustments, but the outcome will be better than you initially thought it would be.

Lion

The lion is a powerful symbol of strength, power, courage, pride, and leadership. No wonder the lion is "king of the jungle." Common expressions, such as *lionhearted* and *he fought like a lion*, indicate this.

The lion has always been associated with the sun. This may be because of its yellow-gold color, or perhaps the shape of the male lion's mane. In ancient Egypt, the lion was associated with Ra and Horus, both solar gods. Aker, a god in the shape of a lion, guarded the gate through which the sun entered the sky every morning.

In Christianity, St. Mark the Evangelist is symbolized by a lion. The lion is also the symbol of the tribe of Judah, and Jesus Christ is sometimes called "the Lion of the tribe of Judah."

Dreaming of a lion means that you're accessing your reserves of inner strength. You will have the necessary confidence, boldness, persistence, and stamina to achieve your goals and will ultimately become extremely successful. If you dream of a pride of lions, you will soon be placed in a leadership role. If you dream of a roaring lion, it's a sign that you'll be taking a stand over a particular issue. It's a sign of new friendships if you dream of lion cubs. It's a sign of a happy home and family life if you dream of a lioness with her cubs. If you win a fight against a lion in your dream, it's a sign that you are overcoming a difficult situation.

If the lion in your dream is terrifying and intimidating, it can indicate someone who is threatening or frightening you. This person is likely to be ruthless, and have little or no consideration for the feelings of others.

If the lion in your dream is running away from you, it's a sign that your pride, confidence, courage, and strength are temporarily deserting you. You will need to regain them as quickly as possible to assert yourself when necessary.

In China, pairs of stone lions are regularly used as guardians of the main entrances to official buildings. The lion on the right-hand side looking out is the male, and the one on the left-hand side is female.

Lizard

Because lizards enjoy basking in the sun, they are often symbolized as souls that are seeking divine light. Consequently, lizards are often found on Greek urns and graves.

Some Christian art also depicts lizards in the same way. Because lizards shed their skins, they are also associated with rebirth, resurrection, and reincarnation.

If you dream of a lizard, it's a sign that you're making changes at a deep, fundamental level that you may not consciously be aware of yet. Your emotions are likely to be heightened, and you may feel anxious or nervous. However, the lizard shows that you're growing and developing, and the outcome will prove positive for you.

See also KOMODO DRAGON.

Locust

Dreaming of locusts is a sign of unexpected fluctuations in fortune. They indicate anxiety, stress, and financial difficulties. However, they also show that you have the ability to change direction quickly when necessary.

Lynx

The mythical lynx was half dog and half panther. It was believed to have extraordinary, penetrating vision. Because of its excellent vision, the ancient Greeks believed it could detect falsehood and even see through walls.

The lynx, as we know it today, is a solitary animal with excellent hearing but only reasonable sight. In medieval times, the lynx was associated with the devil. Native Americans believed the lynx collected secrets and hidden knowledge.

If you dream of a lynx, it's a sign that you should utilize your inner vision to see a situation for what it really is, and then act upon it.

Magpie

In medieval times, artists used the magpie to symbolize evil and death. In Sweden, the magpie was associated with witchcraft. In Devon, people spat three times to avert bad luck when they saw a magpie. In Scotland, people believed that magpies flying near one's home was a sign that someone would shortly die.

An old English rhyme discusses the number of magpies seen:

"One for sorrow, two for joy
Three for a girl, four for a boy,
Five for silver, six for gold,
Seven for a secret never to be told,
Eight for a wish, nine for a kiss,
And ten for a marriage never to be old."

In China, to dream of a magpie is an excellent omen, signifying good news and happiness. It is also considered a sign of a happy marriage. One of the best-loved Chinese legends concerns the cowherd and the weaving maiden. On the seventh day of the seventh moon, magpies gather to create a bridge across the Milky Way. This allows the weaving maiden to visit her lover, the cowherd. On this day, single girls bring offerings to the weaving maiden and have their fortunes told, hoping to learn that their lovers are close at hand.

Two magpies together signify sexual intercourse. Chinese artists frequently paint pictures containing twelve magpies. This traditionally means twelve good wishes.

In the West, magpies are considered thieves, as they are attracted to anything that is shiny. Consequently, dreaming of magpies is a sign that someone is stealing from you. It is considered bad luck to dream of a single magpie, as they mate for life.

Mermaid

The mythical mermaid has the head, arms, and torso of a young woman, and the tail of a fish. Mermaids sit on rocks and sing to passing ships, distracting the sailors and causing them to run their ships aground. Mermaids live at the bottom of the sea, and are reputed to drown men while carrying them down to their lairs.

Mermaids have always been considered unlucky, and are usually a sign of an impending disaster. Dreaming of a mermaid is a sign that you are not fully protected, and someone may try to take advantage of you in some way.

Mink

Mink are territorial, carnivorous mammals that live close to lakes, rivers, and marshes. There are two species: the American and the European. Their glossy fur coats were greatly prized for clothing.

Dreaming of a mink is a sign that a situation may be more complicated than you think. Think matters through before proceeding. It's a sign of a jealous partner if a woman dreams she is wearing a mink coat.

Minotaur

The minotaur is a mythical creature that has become the emblem of Crete. It symbolizes the raw passions of nature. The minotaur is a creature that has the head of a bull on the body of a man. Until he was killed by Theseus, a Greek hero, the minotaur was held captive for nine years in the center of a huge labyrinth built for King Minos.

Because the minotaur was created by the deceit of King Minos, dreaming of a minotaur is a sign that someone is trying to deceive you. Evaluate the important concerns in your life to ensure that everyone involved is acting honestly and ethically.

Mole

The mole is a small, burrowing animal that usually lives in holes underground. Their burrowing creates molehills. Their tiny eyes are able to tell light from dark, but not much else. They rely on their noses, which feel as well as smell. Moles are the only mammals that can use their noses to smell underwater. Because moles live secret, hidden lives underground, it's not surprising that a spy who works in one organization to secretly gain information for another organization is known as a "mole."

Dreaming of a mole is a sign that someone is secretly trying to undermine your position. If you are the mole in your dream, it's a sign that you are trying to undermine someone else. Dreaming of a mole can also indicate a need for time on your own.

Monkey

The monkey is the ninth animal in the Chinese zodiac. In Chinese mythology, gods sometimes appear in the form of monkeys. In the *Ramayana*, the great Indian epic story, the monkey-god, Hanuman, symbolizes kindness, gentleness, loyalty, and self-sacrifice. Early Christians associated monkeys with every possible vice and related them to the devil. The English word *monkey* was not known until 1530, and within a few years it was being used as an affectionate term for playful children.

To dream of monkeys is a sign of pleasant times, enjoyable conversations, and frequent laughter. It relates to the more childlike, mischievous, and playful aspects of the dreamer. Monkeys are sometimes related to adultery, but most of the time the pleasure is innocent fun. To dream of a monkey holding a peach is a sign of longevity.

If you dream of a monkey that is aggressive, or is refusing to hand over something that belongs to you, it's a sign that you've been focusing on a problem that is not as serious or important as you think. When you let go of the problem, the fun will return to your life.

See also APE and CHIMPANZEE.

Moose

The moose is by far the largest member of the deer family. An adult moose stands six and a half feet tall at its shoulder and weighs as much as 1,800 pounds. Its antlers alone weigh about fifty pounds, and can grow an inch a day. The antlers are also extremely sensitive; a moose can detect when a fly lands on them. In Britain, the word *elk* is used for what North Americans call a moose. In the past, moose were hunted for their antlers and meat, but today they are protected animals in both North America and Europe.

Dreaming of a moose is a sign that you'll shortly be faced with a large and unwieldy problem. You'll need to step back and look at it dispassionately. When you do this, the solution will become obvious.

Mouse

The ancient Greeks associated mice with the goddess Aphrodite, because they were considered lascivious. The Romans considered white mice a symbol of good luck. In his dream book, *The Oneirocriticon* (c. 350 CE), the Roman writer Astrampsychus wrote that seeing a mouse in a dream was an extremely propitious sign. During the Middle Ages, people related mice to witches and the souls of dead people. Interestingly, white mice were thought to be the souls of people waiting to be born. Infestations of mice were thought to be divine punishment for some misdeed.

Mice are considered fast-moving, modest, and timid animals. Consequently, dreaming of mice can indicate feelings of embarrassment, timidity, and fear. If mice appear in your dreams, it's a sign that you need to develop more confidence in yourself. However, it also shows that you are single-minded and are quietly progressing towards your goals. It's a sign that you're working well in a group or team if you dream of several mice.

If, in your dream, you experience fear or panic at the sight of a mouse, it's a sign that you're allowing something totally unimportant to destroy your happiness and peace of mind.

If the mice in your dream seem to be pests or vermin, it's a sign that you're overly focused on small concerns and are neglecting the big picture.

Mythical Animals

Mythical and fantastical animals appear relatively frequently in people's dreams. They commonly appear in nightmares. Usually, mythical animals are relatively easy to interpret. Monsters, for instance, symbolize chaos and lack of control. Water monsters symbolize hidden depths, the subconscious, and—sometimes—divine power. Winged animals symbolize esoteric knowledge that the dreamer can discover.

Many mythical animals were first described in the medieval bestiaries that were popular between the eleventh and fourteenth centuries. Although bestiaries were ostensibly books about animals, they were in fact books of Christian morality that were used for religious instruction. Abstinence and chastity were popular themes. Every animal had a moral associated with it, based on the animal's behavior. These books also included stories about plants and even stones.

The earliest bestiary was an anonymous Greek work called *Physiologus*, which dates back to the second century CE. It contains forty-eight chapters, each dealing with a specific animal, plant, or stone. Each is related to a religious text. Because of its popularity, it was translated into many languages, including Anglo-Saxon. All the later bestiaries were based on *Physiologus*, and the symbolism given to different animals is still part of popular folklore today.

The mythical phoenix that burns itself and is born again is a story that originally appeared in *Physiologus*. This book also claims that stags drown their enemies, foxes pretend to be dead in order to entice birds to come near, and hedgehogs use their prickles to collect food for the winter.

Gryphons, unicorns, dragons, and various sea monsters all came from bestiaries.

See also BASILISK, CENTAUR, CERBERUS, DRAGON, ECHIDNA, FURIES, GARGOYLE, GRYPHON, HIPPOG-RIFF, HYDRA, KELPIE, LEVIATHAN, MERMAID, MINO-TAUR, PEGASUS, PHOENIX, SALAMANDER, SATYR, SERPENT, SPHINX, and UNICORN.

Nightingale

An ancient Greek legend tells how Philomena was transformed into a nightingale. Apparently, Tereus, the king of Thrace, invited Philomena to visit his wife. However, when she arrived he raped her, and then cut out her tongue to prevent her from telling anyone about it. However, Philomena told the story by weaving it into a robe, which she sent to Procne, the king's wife. When Procne saw the message in the robe, she cut up her son and fed him to King Tereus. When Tereus learned that he'd eaten his son, he chased Procne all the way to Philomena. The gods were watching this, and transformed all three of them into birds. King Tereus became a hawk; Procne, his wife, became a swallow; and Philomena became a nightingale.

Nightingales are always considered a positive sign that indicates financial success in the near future. If the nightingale is singing, it's a sign of upward progress, such as a promotion or increased responsibility. It's a sign of a quick recovery if you are unwell when you dream of a nightingale. If you're single, dreaming of a nightingale indicates a romance in the near future.

Octopus

The octopus, with its eight tentacles, has always been associated with hell. Early Christians associated it with Satan.

Dreaming of an octopus is a sign of major subconscious conflicts and painful issues that need to be dealt with. The octopus can indicate someone who is able to influence you in many different ways. It can also indicate subconscious fears that are starting to surface. This is a positive sign, since once you are aware of them, you can take appropriate action to resolve them.

Opossum

The humble opossum is one of the world's oldest mammals. It is also the only marsupial found in North America. The main symbolism associated with the opossum is its ability to pretend to be dead. Consequently, if you dream of an opossum it's a sign that you need to stop "playing dead," and confront a problem or situation that needs attention.

Ostrich

In the first century BCE, Pliny the Elder wrote that ostriches bury their heads in the sand. This belief was old even when Pliny wrote about it. However, it's not true. Despite this, if you dream of an ostrich, it's a sign that you're "burying your head in the sand" by trying to avoid a difficult situation. It shows that you need to face up to the situation, and deal with it calmly and rationally. It's a sign of upward progress if, in your dream, you see an ostrich feather lying on the ground.

Otter

Native Americans enjoy the playful aspects of the otter and consider it a trickster. They also associate it with feminine energy, earth, and water.

In China, the otter symbolizes frequent sexual activity. Many Chinese people believed that the male otter is so insatiable that it will make love to a tree when a female partner is not available. Consequently, in the East, to dream of an otter is a sign that your sex life will improve immeasurably.

In the West, the sexual element still applies, but in dreams the otter generally symbolizes nurturing yourself and others. It is a sign of happiness, affection, and well-being.

Owl

In the West, the owl is considered a symbol of wisdom. This belief dates back to the ancient Greeks, who thought the owl's large, expressive eyes, which seldom blink, indicated intelligence. In Greece, owls were sacred to Athena, the goddess of war. However, in peacetime she became the goddess of wisdom. The Romans considered the owl inauspicious. Pliny the Elder even wrote that an entire city could be destroyed if an owl appeared there. Even today, some people in Europe believe someone in the household will die if an owl rests on the roof of their house. The Chinese also consider the owl inauspicious. In the East, it's considered a sign of disaster if you dream of an owl.

Today, most people accept the ancient Greek ideas about the owl. Consequently, if you dream of an owl, it's a sign that you'll gain knowledge, understanding, discernment, and wisdom—either from your own thoughts or intuition, or by seeking advice from someone you trust.

If you dream of an owl while something in your life is coming to an end, it's a sign that you should let go gracefully and not seek to hang on. If you do this, it will be much easier to seize the new starts ahead.

If you hear the hoot of an owl in your dream, it's a sign of a difficult period coming up. You will experience loss, pain, or sadness, but you will come out of the experience a much stronger, more capable person.

Ox

The ox is the emblem of St. Luke and priesthood. A man, lion, eagle, and ox are the four faces of the cherubim (Ezekiel 1:10). Most Nativity scenes include an ox as one of the animals surrounding Jesus in his manger. The ox traditionally symbolizes contentment and nonaggressive strength. The ox is sometimes associated with sacrifice, as it is a castrated bull that has given up its virility to serve its owner.

The ox is the second animal in the Chinese zodiac. The Chinese word *niu* represents the ox, bull, cow, and any other beast of burden. A large number of Chinese people will not eat beef, because it comes from an animal that has helped them bring in their harvest. The ox is associated with home and family, as well as family prosperity.

The ox symbolizes spring. For this reason, to dream of oxen is a good omen, symbolizing new starts, happiness, and joy. Fat oxen indicate upward progress and success. Thin oxen show that your fortunes will decrease. It's also a sign that you will be admired by people of the opposite sex.

See also BULL and COW.

Panda

The panda is a distinctive-looking bear that is native to China. It has black markings around the eyes, ears, and body. Unfortunately, much of its habitat has been destroyed, and it is now an endangered species.

Dreaming of a panda shows that you are adaptable, and can be patient when necessary. It is a sign that all matters in your life will progress slowly in the short term, but everything you learn during this stage will prove helpful in the future.

See also BEAR.

Parrot

Parrots were introduced to the West from India by Alexander the Great. The parrot is often considered a symbol of love. This is because parrots are devoted to their partners and enjoy preening and grooming each other. In ancient Rome, parrots were kept as pets and taught to say phrases such as "Hail, Caesar!" They are still popular as pets today. Parrots are gregarious birds that enjoy communicating with people as well as other birds. A medieval legend says that it was a parrot that announced the coming of the Virgin Mary. The word *popinjay*, as it was used in the Middle Ages, relates to both parrots and the Virgin Mary.[16]

If you dream of a parrot, it's a sign of pleasant times ahead. You will use your verbal skills effectively and will demonstrate tact, sensitivity, and a strong sense of fun in your dealings with others. It also shows that you should relax and make the most of things. If the parrot in your dream is talking incessantly, it's a sign that you're accepting too much on trust. You need to think and evaluate what you hear rather than accepting information and repeating it "parrot" fashion.

Peacock

Because of the peacock's beauty, and doubtless because it spends most of its time on the ground, humans have bred peacocks for thousands of years. In Egypt, the peacock was sacred to the sun god Amun Ra. In Rome, it was sacred to Juno. In India, the peacock is associated with Hindra, the god of thunder. The peacock is one of many animals ridden by Buddha. Early Christians considered the peacock a symbol of immortality and resurrection: immortality, because they believed wrongly that dead peacocks did not decay; and resurrection, because peacocks shed their magnificent feathers every year and grow new ones.

In the West, dreaming of a peacock is a sign of personal satisfaction. You have achieved something worthwhile, and this has bolstered your pride and self-esteem.

In Chinese allegorical painting, the peacock denotes a government official. However, to dream of a peacock means that negative influences are fading away and that happiness is close at hand. The peacock also symbolizes beauty and perfection. For creative people, dreaming of a peacock is also a sign of a literary career.

Pegasus

In Greek mythology, Pegasus is a winged horse that was sired by Poseidon. Every time Pegasus put his hoof on the ground, a healthful spring would be created.

Dreaming of Pegasus is a sign that your spiritual nature is evolving and growing. You are on track, and will shortly gain fresh insights and new opportunities to develop further.

Pelican

The pelican is an interesting bird from a symbolic point of view. At one time it was thought to kill any unattractive offspring, and then restore them to life three days later using blood from self-inflicted wounds. Because of this, it became a symbol of parental love. In medieval times, the story changed slightly. The pelican was said to feed its children with its own blood until it became too weak to continue. It then died. Consequently, it became a symbol of Christ's sacrifice for all humanity. In Christian art, the pelican is considered an emblem of Jesus Christ, as well as a symbol of charity.

If you dream of a pelican, it's a sign that you need to temporarily let go of a plan or idea. It will continue to develop in your subconscious mind until it is ready to be acted upon.

Penguin

Penguins are often considered comical characters in dreams because of their waddling gait when on land or ice. They live in the southern hemisphere, and although most people think they are found only in Antarctica, some live in much more temperate zones. The Galapagos penguin, for instance, lives near the equator.

Penguins appear rarely in people's dreams. If you do happen to dream of penguins, it's a sign that you are suffering from stress and pressure. Although you are managing to handle it, a day or two off would do you a world of good.

Pheasant

In China, the pheasant plays an important role in mythology. The cock is a symbol of cosmic harmony, and the call of the hen is related to *Ch'en* (thunder) in the *I Ching*. The roofs of pagodas are shaped like the wings of flying pheasants.

The pheasant is a symbol of happiness and contentment. Consequently, it's a sign of good fortune in the near future to see a pheasant in your dreams. Pheasants also aid self-understanding and awareness.

Phoenix

The phoenix is a mythical bird that lives for five hundred years. It then flies to Heliopolis, where it is consumed by fire on an altar. Three days later, a young phoenix emerges from the ashes and flies away to live for another five hundred years. For this reason, to rise like a phoenix indicates someone who has failed at something but returns and ultimately triumphs. The phoenix is traditionally considered a sign of resurrection and immortality.

The phoenix has the head of a pheasant, the back of a tortoise, and the tail of a fish. It is brightly colored, and is known as the Vermilion or Red Bird in feng shui. The mythical phoenix is extremely rare. This is possibly because fairies like eating their eggs.[15] It is usually depicted flying, accompanied by many other birds.

The presence of a phoenix in a dream is a sign that you will find new sources of inner strength and achieve prosperity and good harvests. It is a sign of good fortune, protection, and worldly success.

Pig

In ancient times, the pig was the sacred animal of the earth goddess. This is because it was fast growing and prolific, and symbolized a bountiful harvest.[17] Because of its sexual appetite and large number of offspring, the pig was considered a symbol of fertility in Egypt and Greece. The ancient Cretans revered the pig, as Jupiter was suckled by a sow. However, Jews and Muslims consider it an unclean animal. The ancient Celts worshipped the pig and considered pork the ultimate delicacy. Kerridwen and Phaea were sow goddesses. In medieval times, the pig was associated with gluttony, stubbornness, overindulgence, and intemperance.

If you dream of a pig, it is a sign that you need to accept yourself as you are. It indicates a time of transformation, during which your goals and desires will change. If you dream of hunting pigs, it is a sign of victory over obstacles. If the pig in your dream is dirty, gluttonous, and unappealing, it symbolizes someone close to you who is selfish, greedy, mean, and focused on satisfying his or her physical appetite.

More than half of the pigs in the world live in China. The pig is the twelfth and final animal in the Chinese zodiac. It symbolizes virility, and denotes a strong masculine presence in the dreamer's life. In China, pregnant women are given pork to eat, as it is considered to be nourishing for both the mother and fetus. However, knuckle of pork signifies pregnancy, and should not be eaten by virginal young women.

In the East, it is a sign of success to dream of a pig in a test or examination. The dreamer will be honored or rewarded for this feat.

Polar Bear

The polar bear is the largest land carnivore in the world. It lives almost entirely within the Arctic Circle. They are usually solitary animals.

Dreaming of a polar bear is a sign that the situation is unclear, and you run the risk of being deceived by an acquaintance or friend.

See also BEAR.

Porcupine

The porcupine is gentle and looks harmless, but any animal that has been stung by one of its quills is unlikely to attack it again. Porcupines mate for life, and unusually for a rodent, produce only one porcupette, or baby, per litter.

If you dream of a porcupine, it's a sign that you need to treasure the gentle, peace-loving side of your nature but remain aware that there are times when you need to stand up for yourself, to ensure your own needs are being met.

See also HEDGEHOG.

Possum

See OPOSSUM.

Quail

At one time, quails were believed to be extremely amorous, and courtesans were sometimes referred to as "quails."

William Shakespeare referred to this in *Troilus and Cressida* (act 5, scene 1): "Here's Agamemnon, an honest fellow enough, and one that loves quails."

Quail fights, like cockfights, were popular in rural China. Consequently, the quail symbolizes bravery and courage. To dream of a quail shows that you will have the necessary courage to achieve your goals, and should aim higher than you are now. To dream of nine quails means that your descendants will lead happy lives in peace and harmony.

Rabbit
See HARE.

Raccoon
In some Native American traditions, raccoons are considered tricksters. This is because they are determined, voracious, inquisitive, and will do anything to get what they want.

If a raccoon appears in your dreams, it's a sign that you shouldn't succumb to the negative traits of a trickster, such as lying, deception, and talking about people behind their backs. You should accept these feelings, as they are part of you, but you must not act upon them.

Rat
The ancient Egyptians and Phrygians revered rats. The Egyptians felt that rats symbolized good judgment as well as destruction. The Phrygians were impressed that rats always managed to find the freshest bread. Pliny wrote that the ancient Romans considered it a sign of good fortune to see a

white rat. However, anything gnawed by rats indicated bad luck.

Sailors believed that rats deserted a ship that was going to sink. In *The Tempest* (act 1, scene 2), Shakespeare wrote, "The very rats instinctively have quit it."

The rat is the first animal in the Chinese zodiac. In one telling of how this came to be, the ox was at the head of the line when animals were being selected for the zodiac. However, the cunning rat leapt on to the ox's back and jumped off in first position when the animals were being chosen. In most of Asia, the rat symbolizes good luck. In Japan, the rat assists the god of wealth. In Indian mythology, the rat is associated with Ganesh, the Hindu god of wisdom. Artists show this elephant-headed god riding on the back of a rat.

In China, to dream of a rat is a sign of money. The more rats you see, the more money you will receive.

The rat has always had negative connotations in the West, and is related to ill health, witches, and the devil. If you dream of a rat, it's a sign that you're consumed with worry, doubt, and stress at a subconscious level. Something, or someone, is "gnawing" at you, and you will not achieve peace of mind until the situation has been resolved. Rats can also symbolize greed, aggression, and cruelty.

However, rats can survive almost anything. Consequently, to dream of a rat or several rats can be a sign that you will withstand difficult conditions, and will not only survive but thrive as well.

Rats usually appear in dreams when you're involved in an undertaking, usually involving money, and are not sure of the integrity of the other people involved.

Raven

The raven has always been associated with the sun and considered a messenger of the gods. In China and Japan, the raven is thought to provide a connection with the Divine. The ancient Greeks considered the raven sacred to Apollo. The Romans considered the raucous call of the raven a symbol of hope. An old legend says that Cicero (106–43 BCE) was forewarned of his murder by the sound of ravens. One account says they flew into his bedroom and pulled the coverings off his bed. In India, ravens are considered messengers of death. However, in the Bible the raven is considered a symbol of intelligence and vision. Noah sent a raven from the ark to see if the waters were abating. The raven returned without success, but when it was sent again seven days later, it returned with an olive leaf, telling Noah that the waters were subsiding (Genesis 8:6–11).

Because of its color and strange croaking call, the raven is sometimes considered an evil omen and a sign of bad luck. In *Macbeth* (act 1, scene 5), Shakespeare wrote:

"The raven himself is hoarse

That croaks the fatal entrance of Duncan

Under my battlements."

In the Middle Ages, people associated the raven with gluttony. Because ravens live alone, they are often associated with solitude.

Ravens also symbolize the spiritual and mystical side of life. Consequently, they sometimes appear in the dreams of people who are developing psychically or spiritually. In Christian art, ravens symbolize God's providence.

However, dreaming of a raven can also be a warning of impending problems. You'll need to spend time on your own to think about the best way to handle this situation.

Rhinoceros

Powdered rhinoceros horn is a popular aphrodisiac in Asia. This probably came about because it takes rhinoceroses up to an hour to copulate, and the male can ejaculate up to fifty times during that time. The phallic shape of the horn doubtless helps belief in its aphrodisiacal qualities. Early Christian writers were obviously not aware of this aspect of the rhinoceros's reputation. They claimed that the rhino ceased being ferocious and became as gentle as a lamb when in the presence of a virgin.[18]

The rhinoceros used to live in China, and its horn was considered lucky for students. As people who study are believed to possess good character, to dream of a rhinoceros is a sign that the dreamer is developing these qualities. In the West, dreaming of a rhino is a sign that your powerful life force needs to be channelled wisely. When older men dream of a rhino, it's usually a sign that they're mourning lost potency.

Robin

A charming legend attempts to explain the robin's red breast. Apparently, when a robin tried to pull out the thorns from Christ's crown, one stuck in the robin's chest, and the blood stained his breast red. Consequently, the robin is frequently known as "robin redbreast." Another old legend says that robins cover the dead with leaves. While they were doing this for Jesus, their white breasts touched his blood, and they have had red breasts ever since. In the United Kingdom, robins are associated with Christmas and winter. In the United States, robins are associated with spring.

If you dream of a robin, it's a sign that opportunities are starting to open up for you, and you need to evaluate them carefully and seize the ones that are most suitable for you.

Rooster

Because it crows at the break of day, the rooster has always been associated with the sun. It is also a fertility symbol and an emblem of male sexuality. Its reputation as a fertility symbol does not always work to its advantage. Even today, in Europe, its not unusual for freshly cut fields to be fertilized with the blood of a rooster, to ensure the success of the next crop.

If you dream of a rooster, it's a sign that you need to be more open and assertive to obtain what is rightfully yours. A popular one-liner says: "The meek shall inherit the earth after everyone else is finished with it." Be assertive, if necessary, to ensure your own needs are met.

The rooster is the tenth sign of the Chinese zodiac. It is a fortunate animal to dream about, as it traditionally wards off evil and protects the dreamer. It is also a sign of recognition and achievement. A white rooster on a coffin means that demons cannot enter. A red rooster is believed to provide protection against fire. Cockfighting is a popular sport in China, even though it is officially outlawed. Because the rooster is considered such a fortunate animal in China, it is not killed and eaten as it is in the West.

Because chickens have what appears to be a crown on their heads, they are often associated with government and military officials. Consequently, if you dream of a chicken it means you will progress in your career. The same thing applies if you dream of a rooster, but in this case, the promotion will not be a happy one. To dream of chickens fighting in your home is a sign of quarrels and disagreements with other family members.

See also CHICKEN.

Salamander

The salamander is an amphibious, lizardlike animal that usually has moist skin, a slim body, a long tail, and four limbs. However, some salamanders are more eel-like in appearance with missing, or concealed, limbs. Most salamanders are small, but the giant Chinese salamander can grow to almost six feet in length. As salamanders grow, they shed, and eat, the outermost layers of their skin.

The mythical salamander is the one more commonly found in dreams. It is a lizardlike creature that lives in fire. Because of this, Paracelsus (1493–1541), the Swiss physician and writer, associated them with the element of Fire. (He also associated gnomes with Earth, sylphs with Air, and undines with Water.) As the mythical salamander is believed to be sexless, it is associated with chastity. In Christianity, the salamander symbolizes the complete faith of someone who cannot be tempted by the fires of temptation.

Dreaming of a salamander is a sign of purification. You will be eliminating some of the negative aspects of your life, and starting again on a firmer, more solid foundation.

Salmon

Salmon are born in fresh water but then spend time in the ocean before returning home to spawn. So far, no one has been able to explain their remarkable ability to return to the same spot where they were born years before. In Celtic mythology, the salmon is credited with wisdom and sagacity.

Dreaming of salmon is always a positive sign. It shows that you will overcome problems and achieve success. If you are living far away from your birthplace, it's a sign that you should return for a visit.

Satyr

In Greek and Roman mythology, the satyr has the legs, tail, buttocks, and ears of a goat, and the head, arms, and torso of a man. It is a nature spirit who loves women and wine, and is skilful at avoiding work. Because it is considered lazy, lustful, sensuous, and amoral, early Christians associated it with the devil.

Dreaming of a satyr is a sign that you'll be tempted to do something mischievous and slightly out of character. Ensure that other people will not be adversely affected by your actions, and—if it feels right—indulge.

Scorpion

The scorpion was feared in ancient Egypt. However, it was also treated with reverence, and depictions of scorpions exist that possess the head of Isis. According to the Bible, King Rehoboam threatened to chastise his people with scorpions (1 Kings 12:11). In medieval art, scorpions were used to symbolize Satan, as well as death and malice. In Central America, people believed that Mother Scorpion received the souls of the dead at the far end of the Milky Way.

In astrology, Scorpio, or scorpion, is the eighth sign of the zodiac. The sun passes through Scorpio between October 23 and November 21 each year.

There are two main interpretations if you dream of a scorpion. The first is that you may have been hurt (stung) by someone's words or actions. The second is that you may be about to inflict hurt or harm on someone, and should think carefully about your proposed actions.

Seagull

Seagulls are scavenging birds that can be found in coastal regions all around the world. Seagulls are associated with transformation and the ability to handle change effectively. If you dream of seagulls, it's a sign that you're uncertain about some form of change in your life. This will be unsettling for a while, but the seagulls show that you have the necessary strength and understanding to accept, and ultimately welcome, the changes ahead.

Seal

The seal has always played a prominent role in the mythologies of northern people, and selkies are spirits in the mythology of people from the Shetland and Orkney Islands. They appear as seals most of the time, but are also capable of changing into human form. The Celts believed that although fallen angels looked like people on land, they looked like seals in water.

Seals are playful animals. If you dream of a seal, it's a sign that you are taking life far too seriously and should adopt a more playful attitude.

Serpent

The serpent has had a negative reputation ever since one tempted Eve with the forbidden fruit in the Garden of Eden. However, it has also been a symbol of eternity, as it creates a circle by holding its tail in its mouth. The ancient Greeks and Romans considered the serpent a guardian spirit. In the Bible the serpent symbolizes subtlety, wisdom, and the devil:

"Now the serpent was more subtil [*sic*] than any beast of the field which the Lord God had made" (Genesis 3:1).

"Be ye therefore wise as serpents, and harmless as doves" (Matthew 10:16).

In Genesis 3:1–6, the serpent tempts Eve to eat the forbidden fruit.

If you dream of a serpent, it's a sign of repressed energy, usually sexual energy. It usually indicates doubts about desirability and one's own sexuality. Accepting these energies as normal and natural will improve every area of your life.

John Ruskin (1819–1900), the English author and art critic, recorded in his *Diaries* (November 1, 1869) a dream he experienced that involved a serpent: "God restless—taste in my mouth—and had the most horrible serpent dream I ever had yet in my life. The deadliest came out into the room under a door. It rose up like a Cobra—with horrible round eyes and had woman's, or at least Medusa's breasts. It was coming after me, out of one room, like our back drawing room at Herne Hill, into another; but I got some pieces of marble off a table and threw at it, and that cowed it and it went back; but another small one fastened on my neck like a leech, and nothing would pull it off."[19]

See also BASILISK and SNAKE.

Shark

Sharks are powerful and single-minded in achieving their goals. If the shark in your dream is nonthreatening, it's a sign that you should set worthwhile goals and follow your dream.

Sharks usually symbolize fears that are often hidden and just below the surface. Although you might pretend they're not there, eventually you'll have to deal with them. The presence of sharks in your dream is a reminder that you should act sooner rather than later.

If you're sailing over shark-infested seas, you're managing to deal successfully with a difficult situation and will come out of it with your reputation intact.

Sheep

Sheep have been domesticated for approximately nine thousand years.[20] Because they need to be looked after by a shepherd, they came to symbolize weakness, submission, and helplessness. They were also considered pure, which explains why they were so frequently sacrificed in biblical times. The lamb also became a symbol of Christ.

If you dream of a sheep, it's a sign that you need to leave the "flock," and think for yourself. If you dream of sheep and wolves, you're being tempted to do something that you normally wouldn't do. Sheep and wolves, as well as sheep and goats, symbolize good and evil.

Dreaming of a lamb or lambs is a sign of innocence and purity. The apparent weakness, childlike nature, and vulnerability of the lamb gives you the ability to overcome evil.

If you dream of a flock of sheep, it's a sign that you have been accepted into a group or organization.

The sheep is the eighth animal in the Chinese zodiac. Because the lamb kneels when it is being suckled, the sheep became a symbol of strong family feelings, especially love for the parents. In China, to dream of sheep is a sign of a strong, stable, nurturing family unit.

Snail

Snails are sluglike animals with a shell. Because they move slowly, snails have always been considered a symbol of laziness. Someone who works at a "snail's pace" is making slow progress.

Dreaming of a snail means that you are deliberately making slow progress, probably to confound or confuse others. If you are walking on snails in your dream, it's a sign that you'll have to deal with unpleasant people in the near future.

Snake

Snakes appear in people's dreams more commonly than any other animal. There are probably more fears, phobias, and superstitions about snakes than all other animals combined. Native Americans associate snakes with healing and transformation. The ancient Romans also associated them with healing, as a snake was the symbol of Asclepius, the god of medicine and healing. Even today, the symbol of medicine is the caduceus, a staff with two snakes entwined around it. The caduceus was originally carried by Mercury, messenger of the gods.

If you dream of a snake, it's a sign that your subconscious mind is trying to communicate with your conscious mind. A snake in the grass is a sign that someone is trying to undermine you. At the very least, this person is disloyal. If you dream that the snake is entwined around you, it's a sign that you are hemmed in, restricted, or trapped in some way. If you dream of a snake with its tail in its mouth, you are trying to harmonize the spiritual and physical sides of your makeup. A snake biting you is a sign that you are poisoning yourself with your own thoughts and emotions.

The snake is the fifth animal in the Chinese zodiac. In Chinese prehistory, snakes were worshipped, but they gradually came to symbolize treachery and evil. Consequently, dream interpretations vary, depending on what the snake is doing. It is a sign of good luck if a snake chases you in a dream. To dream of a black snake indicates the birth of a girl, while a white or grey snake indicates a boy. If a man dreams about a single snake, it is a sign that he will shortly have a new girlfriend. In Taiwan it is believed that if you dream of a snake coiling itself around you, you will shortly experience an important change in your life.

In the West, it's considered a positive sign to dream of a snake, despite the negative connotations the snake has in the Judeo-Christian tradition. Dreaming of a snake encourages you to find your true purpose. The snake sheds off its own skin many times in its life. This signifies a new start, both for you and the snake. Many people are scared of snakes, but in the dream world to be bitten by a snake is a sign that you're being forced into a new, more positive direction.

The snake has always had sexual, especially phallic, associations. It's a sign of strong masculine energy if a woman dreams of a snake in her bedroom.

If you kill a snake in a dream, it's a sign that you'll overcome your enemies.

A threatening snake is an indication that a difficult situation could be hard to control.

See also SERPENT.

Sparrow

Sparrows are small, brown-grey birds that eat almost anything. They are scavengers and have the ability to adapt to almost any environment.

Dreaming of a sparrow is a sign that you will not only survive, but you will also thrive. You are sympathetic, understanding, and patient. You deserve happiness, and are able to overcome any obstacle or misfortune that comes your way.

Sphinx

The Egyptian sphinx had the body of a lion and the head of a pharaoh. It was a symbol of regal power. In Greek mythology, the sphinx was a mythical creature with a human head (usually female), a bull's body, the wings of an eagle, and the feet of a lion. It had a human's voice. The sphinx is extremely wise and symbolizes the riddle of the universe. In fact, the sphinx was an expert on riddles, and enjoyed asking riddles to people who came to the Greek city of Thebes. If they could not answer, she would eat them. The sphinx killed herself after Oedipus solved the riddle he was asked: "What goes on four legs in the morning, two legs at noon, and three legs in the evening?" The answer is "man."

If you dream of a sphinx, it's a sign that you need to ask an important question. Although you probably already know the answer, it's important that you ask the question.

Spider

Early Christians considered the spider a symbol of Satan, who constantly tries to lead people into his web of sin. The Navajo people believe spiders taught people the art of weaving. Because of its ability to spin webs, the spider is usually considered a symbol of creativity. In effect, it is telling you to weave the fabric of your life in your own unique way. Superstitious people still believe that it is good luck to find a small spider on your clothes. Extremely small spiders are called money spiders and are a sign that money is coming.

Dreaming of spiders is a call to action. It shows that you need to make a major decision. You'll have many opportunities, and will need to think carefully, before choosing one and following it through.

It's a sign of sexual repression and a fear of intimacy if you dream of a spider in your bed. If possible, discuss the dream with your partner, and see if the dream reoccurs. With love and goodwill on both sides, these dreams will become less frequent and will ultimately disappear.

Squirrel

The squirrel has not fared well in Christian symbolism. Because it stores up food, Christians considered it a symbol of greed. In the Middle Ages, the squirrel was associated with the devil because of its speed and rapid, darting movements. In Germanic mythology, the squirrel lived in Yggdrasil, the world ash tree, and was sacred to Thor, the god of thunder and rain.

If you dream of a squirrel, it's a sign that you're "squirreling" away information but are not making practical use of it. As squirrels are always busy and quick moving, squirrels can also indicate that you're focused on a particular task and will finish it as quickly as you can. However, this busy-ness needs to be used productively, as otherwise you may end up being endlessly busy but have little to show for it.

Stag

The stag is a male deer, sometimes known as a *hart*. It has fascinated people for thousands of years, because its antlers are renewed every year. Cave paintings, dating from the Paleolithic period, frequently depict stags, as well as people wearing antlers and the skins of stags. The ancient Celts believed that stags acted as a guide to souls and helped them move into the next world.

Animals with horns are traditionally linked with male sexuality. Because of this, horns are frequently ground to powder and used as aphrodisiacs. For the same reason, stags are also associated with fertility, potency, passion, and power.

However, during the Middle Ages, the stag was considered a sign of purity. Both St. Eustace (early second century CE) and St. Hubert (656–727) were said to have become Christians after seeing a glowing crucifix between the antlers of a stag. King Richard II (1367–1400) used a white stag as his emblem.

Because stags are solitary animals, they have also become a symbol of loneliness and melancholy.

To dream of a stag is usually a sign of repressed sexuality. However, it can also be a sign of self-enforced loneliness that is continuing too long for your mental well-being.

See also DEER.

Starfish

The starfish symbolizes regeneration, as it is has the ability to regrow missing limbs. Dreaming of starfish is an extremely positive sign, as they also symbolize hope. It is a sign that your life is steadily improving.

Stork

The stork was sacred to Juno, the Roman goddess who protected women, marriage, and family. The popular image of a stork delivering a human baby probably dates from this association. Christians associated the stork with Christ's resurrection, as spring began as soon as the stork returned from its winter migration. In Sweden, the stork was considered sacred because Swedes believed it flew around the cross of Christ, calling out, "Styrka, Styrka!" which means "Strength, strength!"

It is a sign of changes in your life if you dream of a stork. These changes can include parenthood, if that is your goal. If the stork is sitting on its nest, it's a sign of family difficulties that will prove worrisome but will be short lived.

Swallow

The swallow has widely varying interpretations in different parts of the world. The ancient Greeks considered the swallow a sign of bad luck, while the Romans considered it highly auspicious. The Chinese considered it a symbol of courage and initiative, but the Japanese thought it a sign of unfaithfulness. It has always been considered unlucky to kill a swallow. John Dryden (1631–1700), the English poet, wrote:

"Perhaps you fail'd in your fore-seeing skill,

For *swallows* are unlucky birds to kill." (*The Hind and the Panther*, part III)

The swallow is usually considered a sign of spring, since the birds return to the same spot they left from each year after their annual migration. Probably the most famous example of this are the swallows that traditionally return to the Mission of San Juan Capistrano in California on March 19th every year.

To dream of a swallow is a sign of great happiness, children, and pleasant activities.

Swan

Swans have always symbolized grace, dignity, and elegance. In Greek mythology, swans pull Apollo's chariot. Another Greek myth says that the soul of Apollo entered into a swan, and ever since, the soul of every good poet has passed into a swan. Because of its pure white color, the Greeks also associated the swan with purity and chastity. Interestingly, they also associated the swan with the gift of prophecy, and believed it could foretell its own death. In the Middle Ages, the pure and chaste aspects of the white swan, along with its beauty, made it a symbol of the Virgin Mary. Not surprisingly, the black swan became associated with Satan. An old story, dating back to Plato and Aristotle, says that swans sing beautifully when they are about to die.

If you dream of a white swan swimming in the water, it's a sign that you're accomplishing your goals in a smooth, efficient, and seemingly effortless manner. If you dream of a black swan, you'll also achieve your goals, but it will take a great deal of time and effort.

Tiger

Because the tiger was unknown in the West until early Christian times, most of the symbology associated with it comes from the East. Kali, the Hindu goddess of creation and destruction, rode a tiger. Shiva, the Destroyer god, wears a tiger skin. The tiger and the dragon play a major role in the Form School of feng shui.[21] The tiger and the dragon are also the two irresistible forces in Buddhism. The tiger is the third animal in the Chinese zodiac. It symbolizes bravery, steadfastness, and courage. It is also believed to be able to drive away demons, which is why stone tigers are sometimes found on gravestones.

To dream of a tiger is a sign that you will shortly be tested, and will need to be honest, confident, and courageous. You will have to stand up for yourself, or for someone or something you believe in. If you succeed in this, you will be recognized and promoted. It is a good omen to dream of escaping from a tiger, as this means you will shortly hear good news.

The Ao Naga people of northeastern India believe that if a young girl dreams that a tiger is following her, it is a sure sign that a young man is in love with her. People of the Angami Naga tribe believe that if a betrothed couple dream of a tiger, the marriage will be an extremely fortunate one.[22] In Java, any dreams that include tigers are a sign of good luck, and indicate that respect and high status will come to the dreamer.[23]

Toad

The toad usually has negative connotations. People believed that touching one gave you warts, and looking at their eyes could make you epileptic. People also believed toads were an important ingredient in witches' brews. In Egypt, the toad symbolized death. In the Middle Ages, the toad became a symbol of lust and licentiousness, especially in Christian art.

One hundred and two cane toads were brought from Hawaii to Australia in 1935 to control the cane beetle, which was destroying the sugar cane crops. The exercise proved a disaster, and there are now more than one hundred million cane toads in Australia. Cane toads are venomous—and eating them as eggs, tadpoles, or toads means instant death for most animals. Their poison even kills crocodiles.

The toad is considered a sign of longevity in the East. An old story claims that toads contain a precious jewel inside their heads. William Shakespeare referred to this when he wrote:

"Sweet are the uses of adversity,

Which, like the toad, ugly and venomous,

Wears yet a precious jewel in its head." (*As You Like It*, act 2, scene 1.)

In the East, dreaming of a toad is an indication of a long, happy life and many sons. In the West, dreaming of a toad is a sign that you need to develop more self-belief and act more confidently.

See also FROG.

Tortoise

The ancient Egyptians had a tortoise god called Apesh who was associated with black magic and evil. In ancient Greece, the tortoise was associated with Aphrodite, most probably because of its fertility. In Africa, the tortoise symbolizes knowledge and power. It is also considered something of a trickster, who can do both good and bad. The tortoise has always been a highly symbolic animal in China. At one time it was believed that gods lived inside the shells of tortoises and turtles.[24] In the Chinese tradition, the tortoise supported the world, and its four feet indicated the four corners of the earth.

Tortoises symbolize wisdom, stability, longevity, and the ability to withstand anything the fates toss in their direction. It also means progressing at your own pace. To dream of tortoises mean that you will survive and thrive, no matter what the current situation appears to be like.

See also TURTLE.

Toucan

Toucans are brightly colored birds with large bills. They are found in Central America and South America, as well as the Caribbean. In parts of South America, the toucan has been associated with evil spirits, and some people believe the birds are reincarnated demons. However, the toucan is also considered a tribal totem, and medicine men fly on them to reach the spirit world.

Dreaming of a toucan shows you can move freely in many different worlds. You can make your presence felt when necessary, and it will soon be time for you to take a stand and speak your mind.

Turkey

Turkeys are arguably best known for their role in Thanksgiving dinners. They are native to North America. They received their name because they were misidentified by European settlers, who incorrectly thought turkeys were another type of what were then sometimes called *turkey fowl,* also known as *guinea fowl*, due to those birds being imported to Europe via Turkey.

Dreaming of a live turkey is a sign that business and financial prospects are good. If you are eating turkey in your dream, it's a sign of happiness in the near future.

Turtle

Turtles have the same basic meanings as tortoises. However, as turtles live on both land and water, they symbolize the capacity to think logically and feel deeply simultaneously. The hard shell of tortoises and turtles symbolizes the ability to protect yourself from the verbal and physical attacks of others.

See also TORTOISE.

Unicorn

The mythical unicorn is a horselike animal with a single horn in the middle of its forehead. Unicorns were first described by Ctesias, the Greek historian and physician, in about 400 BCE. According to legend, the only person who can catch a unicorn is a virgin. Unicorns were said to be able to detect poison by dipping their horns into any suspect food or drink. A unicorn is safe if it jumps into a virgin's lap while being pursued. Because of this, the Virgin Mary is often depicted with a unicorn in her lap, to symbolize the Immaculate Conception.

The unicorn symbolizes purity and goodness. It also traditionally represents a large and happy family. In China, this meant many sons, and the unicorn is sometimes shown in Chinese art with a young boy on its back.

To dream of a unicorn is a sign of many pleasant family activities. If a young woman dreams of a unicorn, it indicates a son in her near future.

Vulture

In ancient Egypt, the vulture protected the pharaohs, and the queen's necklace depicted a vulture. Nekhbet, the guardian goddess of Upper Egypt, was frequently depicted as a vulture. According to Greek mythology, Zeus was able to transform himself into a vulture. In Roman mythology, the vulture was sacred to Mars, the god of war, and it was an offense to kill one. Early Christians associated the vulture with virginity, as they believed the eggs were fertilized by the east wind. Not surprisingly, the vulture became associated with the Virgin Mary. The Mayans considered the vulture a symbol of death.

If you dream of a vulture, it's a sign that something is coming to an end, but something better will evolve as a result. The knowledge gained from the experience that is ending will prove helpful to you in the future.

Weasel

Weasels rarely appear in dreams. They symbolize subtlety and flexibility. Dreaming of a weasel is a sign that you should be cautious about a current situation. Focus on your goal. Be as flexible as necessary and move quickly when the time is right.

If you dream about an angry or unpleasant weasel, it's a sign that someone is not telling you all the facts. Be careful before committing yourself to any course of action, and refuse to sign anything without receiving professional advice first.

Whale

Whales can be found in all the oceans of the world. They vary in size from eleven feet to more than one hundred feet in length. In Chinese mythology, a giant whale with the hands and feet of a man was said to rule the oceans. The famous story of Jonah being swallowed by a whale is found in both the Bible and the Koran.

Dreaming of a whale is a sign that you have successfully left the past behind and are revealing your true inner self, possibly for the first time since you were a young child. The whale symbolizes promise, hope, and a strong desire to make the future as good as you possibly can. You have the potential, power, and ability to succeed at anything you attempt.

Wolf

Romulus and Remus, the legendary founders of Rome, were suckled by a she-wolf who became the symbol of Rome. In Greek mythology, the wolf is associated with Apollo, the god of light, healing, and prophecy. Native Americans have always respected the wolf, and sometimes name themselves after them. They consider the wolf an emblem of strength, stamina, and stealth. In the Christian tradition, the wolf is associated with Satan and the lamb with Jesus. However, the wolf is also an emblem of St. Francis, who is reputed to have tamed a wolf called Gubbio.

In the West, the wolf symbolizes greed, cruelty, and revenge. To dream of a wolf is a warning that someone will not be what he or she appears to be, and that the dreamer needs to take steps to avoid becoming a victim. If you over-come or defeat a wolf in a dream, it is a sign that you'll overcome anything that stands in the way of your goal. If a wolf bites you in your dream, it is a sign that someone is working against you. A howling wolf is a sign that someone close to you needs your help. A pack of wolves indicates a fear that someone is cheating you.

Wolves can also symbolize our baser animal instincts. If you dream of an aggressive wolf, it is a sign of sexual re-pression.

However, wolves also have a positive side, which is why people often choose them as their totem animal. Wolves can indicate a need to stay true to yourself, to remain fo-cused on your goals, and to turn away from addictive or compulsive behaviors.

Woodpecker

Woodpeckers live in forests and wooded areas in most countries of the world. The more than two hundred spe-cies of woodpeckers range in size from three and a quarter inches to twenty inches in length.

Dreaming of a woodpecker is a sign that someone or something is trying to catch your attention. You will need to listen carefully to find out what it is.

Zebra

Zebras are sociable animals with distinctive black and white stripes. They are native to Africa. In Namibia, a folktale says that zebras were originally white. However, during a disagreement with a baboon over a waterhole, the zebra kicked the baboon and fell over into a fire that left scorch marks all over his white coat.

Dreaming of a zebra is a sign that you retain your individuality at all times, even inside a group of like-minded people.

Conclusion

I hope this book has encouraged you to start paying more attention to the animals in your dreams. You'll find the insights you gain from them helpful in everyday life, and they may even prove rewarding in other ways.

Wilbur Wright, an English author, experienced a number of telepathic dreams. Three of them—in 1946, 1951, and 1954—involved horse races, which was surprising because Wilbur had never been to a racecourse. In each dream, Wilbur asked someone standing beside him which horse had won the "big race." On the first occasion, he was told that a horse named Airborne had won. He later discovered that a horse named Airborne was racing and the odds were sixty-six to one. He told a few friends about his dream, but none of them made a bet. As Wilbur was not interested in horse racing, he didn't bother to bet either. They must all have been annoyed with themselves when Airborne won.

Five years later, Wilbur dreamt an almost identical dream. On this occasion, the same person was standing next to him in the dream and told him that Arctic Prince would win the Epsom Derby. This time his friends bet on the horse and did extremely well, as Arctic Prince won. Again, Wilbur didn't bother to place a bet.

In 1954, Wilbur had the same dream yet again. However, on this occasion, the dream turned into a lucid one and Wilbur realized he was dreaming. When he noticed the same companion was standing beside him, he said, "Oh no! Not you again!" This time, the man told him that a horse named Radar would win. When Wilbur woke up, he discovered there was no horse named Radar racing on the following day. However, there was a horse named Nahar running at the Lincolnshire Handicap, and the lady he was staying with placed a bet. Naturally, Nahar won, but yet again, Wilbur had not placed a bet.[1]

Although Wilbur Wright did not take advantage of his precognitive animal dreams, there are many recorded instances in which people did make money as a result of their dreams.

In 1946, a young Oxford University student named John Godley woke up after dreaming that two horses had won their races. A group of his friends decided to place a bet. Both horses won, and John's share was more than one hundred pounds. A few weeks later, he had another dream, which he told to his brother and sister. They placed a bet, and made more than sixty pounds. A few months later, he had another precognitive dream, and again his horse won. John's dreams continued, but not all of them provided winners. In 1958, John won four hundred and fifty pounds on a horse, but that was his last major win. On the strength of his successful dreams, the *Daily Mirror* asked him to become their racing journalist.[2]

Most people's dreams about animals do not involve horse races. Not surprisingly, dreams about winning money are well documented, as everyone loves the idea of making some easy money. Virtually all animal dreams are much more important than winning money, though, as they provide valuable insights and advice that enhance the lives of the people who experience them.

I hope the information in this book will enhance and enrich your life.

Notes

Introduction

1. The Zapotecs of Mexico have a different way of determining an unborn child's spirit animal. When the mother is about to give birth, her relatives draw a number of different animals on the floor of the hut. They then erase them, one by one. Whatever animal has not been erased by the time the baby is born becomes his or her spirit animal. See Yvonne Aburrow, *The Magical Lore of Animals* (Chieveley, UK: Capall Bann Publishing, 2000), 12.

2. Goh Kheng Yew and Wong Wai Kan, *The Sage and the Butterfly: A Guide to Chinese Dream Interpretation* (Singapore: Rank Books, 2001), 15.

3. *The New Encyclopaedia Britannica, Macropaedia*, vol. 5 (Chicago: Encyclopaedia Britannica, Inc., 1983), 1011.

4. The Bible contains descriptions of many dreams, including the dream of Abimelech (Genesis 20:3–8); the dreams of Pharaoh's butler and baker (Genesis 40:5–19); Pharaoh's dream about seven good years, followed by seven bad years (Genesis 41:1–36); the dream of the Midianite (Judges 7:13–15); the dream of Solomon (1 Kings 3:5–15); Nebuchadnezzar's dreams (Daniel 2:1–49); and Joseph's dreams (Matthew 1:20–24 and Matthew 2:13).

5. Plato, *The Republic, Book IX*, trans. by Benjamin Jowett, 1892. Numerous editions available.

6. Steven Starker, PhD, *Fantastic Thought* (Englewood Cliffs, NJ: Prentice-Hall, 1982), 8.

7. Donald R. Goodenough, "Dream Recall: History and Current Status of the Field," in *The Mind in Sleep: Psychology and Psychophysiology*, edited by A. Arkin, J. Antrobus, and S. Ellman (Secaucus, NJ: Lawrence Erlbaum and Associates, 1978), 130.

8. Willard Z. Park, *Shamanism in Western North America: A Study of Cultural Relationships* (Evanston, IL: Northwestern University, 1938), 83.

9. *The Jívaro: People of the Sacred Waterfalls* (Garden City, NY: Doubleday/Natural History Press, 1972), 138–39.

Chapter One

1. Ian Oswald, *Sleep*, revised edition (Harmondsworth, UK: Penguin, 1970), 67.

2. Ibid., 68.

3. Carl G. Jung, quoted in Fraser Boa, *The Way of the Dream: Conversations on Jungian Dream Interpretation with Marie-Louise von Franz* (Boston: Shambhala Publications, 1992), 70.

4. Fraser Boa, *The Way of the Dream*, 84.

5. Robert Stickgold, quoted in "Dreams Can Fix Memory: Scientists," unattributed article in *The New Zealand Herald* (Auckland), April 27, 2010. The original findings were published in Erin J. Wamsley, Matthew Tucker, Jessica D. Payne, Joseph A. Benavides, and Robert Stickgold, "Dreaming of a Learning Task Is Associated with Enhanced Sleep-Dependent Memory Consolidation," *Current Biology*, vol. 20, issue 9 (April 2010). Abstract online at http://www.cell.com/current-biology/abstract/S0960-9822(10)00352-0.

6. Alan Vaughan, PhD, "Intuitive Dreaming," *Intuition* magazine (Mountain View, CA: Intuitive Media), August 1996, 10.

Chapter Three

1. Emil Preetorius, *Kunst des Ostens: Sammlung Preetorius* [Art of the East: The Preetorius Collection]. (Munich: Staatliches Museum für Völkerkunde, 1958).

2. Carl G. Jung, *Man and His Symbols* (New York: Arkana, 1990), 20. Originally published by Aldus Books in 1964.

3. Ong Hean-Tatt, *Chinese Animal Symbolisms* (Petaling Jaya, Malaysia: Pelanduk Publications, 1993), 9–10.

4. K. C. Chang, *Art, Myth and Ritual: The Path to Political Authority in Ancient China* (Cambridge, MA: Harvard University Press, 1983), 74.

5. Ong Heann-Tatt, *Chinese Animal Symbolisms*, 28–33.

6. Aniela Jaffé, "Symbolism in the Visual Arts," part 4 of Carl G. Jung, *Man and His Symbols* (first published in 1964).

7. Richard Webster, *Is Your Pet Psychic?* (St. Paul, MN: Llewellyn Publications, 2002). This book contains a variety of experiments that are designed to help you communicate psychically with your pet.

Chapter Four

1. *Encyclopaedia Britannica, 15th ed., Macropaedia 18,* (Chicago: Encyclopaedia Britannica, Inc., 1974), 529.

2. C. A. Burland, "Totem," in Richard Cavendish, et. al., eds., *Man, Myth & Magic: The Illustrated Encyclopedia of Mythology, Religion, and the Unknown* (London: Marshall Cavendish Corporation, 1970), 2859.

3. Joseph L. Henderson, in Neil Russack, *Animal Guides in Life, Myth and Dreams* (Toronto: Inner City Books, 2002), 7.

4. Joel Rothschild, *Signals: An Inspiring Story of Life After Life* (Novato, CA: New World Library, 2000), 83.

Chapter Five

1. Miranda and Stephen Aldhouse-Green, *The Quest for the Shaman: Shape-Shifters, Sorcerers and Spirit Healers in Ancient Europe* (London: Thames & Hudson Limited, 2005), 17 and 44.

2. Margaret Murray, *The Witch-Cult in Western Europe* (Oxford: Oxford University Press, 1921). Chapter VIII: "Familiars and Transformations." Available online at http://www.sacred-texts.com/pag/wcwe/wcwe08.htm

3. James George Frazer, *The Golden Bough: A Study in Magic and Religion* (London: Macmillan and Company, 1922), 687.

4. There are many translations of Amairgen's poem. This version is from *The Irish Mythological Cycle* by H. D'Arbois de Jubainville (Dublin: Hodges, Figgis and Company, 1903). It is a translation of his *L'Épopée Celtique en Irlande* (Paris, 1884).

5. Nandor Fodor, *Encyclopaedia of Psychic Science* (New Hyde Park, NY: University Books, 1966), 209–10. Originally published in 1934.

6. Nandor Fodor, "Lycanthropy as a Psychic Mechanism," *Journal of American Folk-Lore*, vol. 58 (1945), 310–16. Reprinted in William R. Corliss, *The Unfathomed Mind: A Handbook of Unusual Mental Phenomena* (Glen Arm, MD: The Sourcebook Project, 1982), 70–71.

7. Robert Eisler, "Therianthropy," in Edward Podolsky, ed., *Encyclopedia of Aberrations: A Psychiatric Handbook* (New York: Philosophical Library, 1953), 523.

8. Juba Kennerley, *The Terror of the Leopard Men* (London: Stanley Paul and Company, 1940), 14.

9. J. H. Hutton, *The Sema Nagas* (Oxford: Oxford University Press, 1968), 271–73. Originally published in London by Macmillan and Company, 1921.

10. Herbert T. White, *A Civil Servant in Burma.* (London: Edward Arnold Limited, 1913), 301.

11. J. A. MacCulloch, "Lycanthropy," in J. Hastings, ed., *Encyclopaedia of Religion and Ethics*, vol. 8 (New York: Charles Scribner's Sons, 1916), 210.

12. Helen Churchill Candee, *New Journeys in Old Asia* (New York: Frederick A. Stokes Company, 1927), 63–64.

13. J. B. H. Thurston, "Tiger! Tiger!" *Natural History Magazine*, vol. 44, number 4 (1939), 241–45.

14. Arthur Locke, *The Tigers of Trengganu* (London: Museum Press Limited, 1954), 157.

15. Robert Wessing, *The Soul of Ambiguity: The Tiger in Southeast Asia* (DeKalb, IL: Northern Illinois University, 1986), 14–15.

Chapter Six

1. L. G. Cashmore, *Dogs That Serve* (London: George Ronald, 1960), 130.

2. Verité Reily Collins, *999 and Other Working Dogs* (York, UK: WSN, 2005), 20.

3. Peter Browne, "The Healing Power of Pets," *Reader's Digest* (Asian edition), August 2000.

4. Erika Friedmann, Aaron H. Katcher, Sue A. Thomas, James J. Lynch, and Peter R. Messent, "Animal Companions and One-Year Survival of Patients after Discharge from a Coronary Care Unit," *Public Health Report 95* (1980), 307–12.

5. Deborah Halber, "Animals Have Complex Dreams," *MIT News*, January 31, 2001. Online at http://mit .edu/newsoffice/2001/dreams-0131.html. Also see Deborah Halber, "Picower Researcher Explains How Rats Think," *MIT News*, February 12, 2006, http://web.mit.edu/newsoffice/2006/instant-replay.html; and Deborah Halber, "Memory Experts Show Sleeping Rats May Have Visual Dreams," *MIT News*, December 18, 2006. Online at http://web.mit .edu/newsoffice/2006/visual-cortex.html.

Chapter Seven

1. Joseph Banks, *Journal of the Right Hon. Sir Joseph Banks During Captain Cook's First Voyage in H.M.S. Endeavour in 1768–71 to Terra del Fuego, Otahite, New Zealand, Australia, the Dutch East Indies, etc.* (London: Macmillan and Company, 1896), 63. This book is also available free on several sites online.

2. Marie-Louise von Franz, *A Psychological Interpretation of the Golden Ass of Apuleius* (Irving, TX: Spring Publications, 1980), 122.

3. Enos A. Mills, *In Beaver World.* (Lincoln: University of Nebraska Press, 1990), 78–80. Originally published in 1913.

4. Fang Jing Pei and Zhang Juwen, *The Interpretation of Dreams in Chinese Culture* (Trumbull, CT: Weatherhill, Inc., 2000), 49.

5. Joseph L. Henderson, "Ancient Myths and Modern Man," in Carl G. Jung, *Man and His Symbols* (New York: Dell Publishing, 1968), 131–32.

6. Patricia Dale-Green, *Cult of the Cat* (Boston: Houghton Mifflin, 1963), 18–19.

7. Wolfram Eberhard, *A Dictionary of Chinese Symbols* (London: Routledge and Kegan Paul Limited, 1986), 58–59. Originally published as *Lexicon Chinesischer Symbole* (Köln, Germany: Eugen Diederichs Verlag, 1983.)

8. *Encyclopaedia Britannica, 15th ed., Micropaedia II* (Chicago: Encyclopaedia Britannica, Inc., 1983), 1031.

9. Elizabeth Caspari with Ken Robbins, *Animal Life in Nature, Myth and Dreams* (Wilmette, IL: Chiron Publications, 2003), 61.

10. J. C. Cooper, *Symbolic and Mythological Animals* (London: HarperCollins, 1992), 92–93.

11. Frederick Greenwood, *Imagination in Dreams* (London: John Lane, 1894), 196.

12. David Fontana, *The Secret Language of Symbols* (San Francisco: Chronicle Books, 1993), 94.

13. Artemidorus, *The Interpretation of Dreams,* trans., Robert White (Park Ridge, NJ: Noyes Press, 1975), 121.

14. Anna Kavan (pseudonym of Helen Woods), "A Visit," short story in *Julia and the Bazooka* (London: Peter Owen Limited, 1970).

15. C. A. S. Williams, *Outlines of Chinese Symbolism* (New York: Dover Publications, 1976), 324. This is a reprint of the third revised edition, originally published by Kelly and Walsh Limited, in Shanghai, China, in 1941. (The first edition, printed by Customs College Press, in Peiping [Beijing], China, was published in 1931.)

16. Bruce Thomas Boehrer, *Parrot Culture: Our 2500-Year-Long Fascination with the World's Most Talkative Bird* (Philadelphia: University of Pennsylvania Press, 2004), 37.

17. Marija Gimbutas, *The Civilization of the Goddess* (San Francisco: HarperSanFrancisco, 1991), 229.

18. Carl G. Jung, *Collected Works, Volume 11* (Princeton, NJ: Princeton University Press, 1977), 408.

19. John Ruskin (selected and edited by Joan Evans and John Howard Whitehouse), *The Diaries of John Ruskin 1848–1873* (Oxford: Oxford University Press, 1958), vol. 2, 267.

20. Ronald John Nowak, *Walker's Mammals of the World, Volume II* (Baltimore, MD: John Hopkins University Press, 1991), 1408.

21. Richard Webster, *Feng Shui for Beginners* (St. Paul, MN: Llewellyn Publications, 2002), 22.

22. Richard Webster, *Feng Shui for Success & Happiness* (St. Paul, MN: Llewellyn Publications, 1999), 2.

23. J. P. Mills, *The Ao Nagas* (London: Macmillan and Company Limited, 1926), 294.

24. Robert Wessing, *The Soul of Ambiguity: The Tiger in Southeast Asia* (DeKalb, IL: Northern Illinois University, 1986), 53.

Conclusion

1. Colin Wilson, *Beyond the Occult* (London: Guild Publishing, 1988), 154–55.

2. Colin Wilson, *Mysteries* (London: Hodder & Stoughton Limited, 1978), 147–49.

Suggested Reading

Aburrow, Yvonne. *The Magical Lore of Animals*. Chieveley, UK: Capall Bann Publishing, 2000.

Aldhouse-Green, Miranda, and Stephen Aldhouse-Green. *The Quest for the Shaman*. London: Thames & Hudson, 2005.

Andrews, Ted. *Animal Speak*. St. Paul, MN: Llewellyn Publications, 1993.

———. *Animal-Wise*. Jackson, TN: Dragonhawk Publishing, 1999.

———. *The Art of Shapeshifting*. Jackson, TN: Dragonhawk Publishing, 2005.

Artemidorus (translated by Robert White), *The Interpretation of Dreams*. Park Ridge, NJ: Noyes Press, 1975.

Bowater, Margaret M. *Dreams and Visions: Language of the Spirit*. Auckland, New Zealand: Tandem Press, 1997.

Caspari, Elizabeth, with Ken Robbins. *Animal Life in Nature, Myth and Dreams.* Wilmette, IL: Chiron Publications, 2003.

Clark, Joseph D. *Beastly Folklore.* Metuchen, NJ: The Scarecrow Press, 1968.

Cowan, James G. *The Elements of the Aborigine Tradition.* Shaftesbury, UK: Element Books Limited, 1992.

Eisler, Robert. *Man into Wolf: An Anthropological Interpretation of Sadism, Masochism, and Lycanthropy.* London: Routledge and Kegan Paul Limited, 1951.

Frazer, James George. *The Golden Bough: A Study in Magic and Religion.* London: Macmillan and Company, 1922.

Gongloff, Robert P. *Dream Exploration: A New Approach.* Woodbury, MN: Llewellyn Publications, 2006.

Guiley, Rosemary Ellen. *Dreamspeak: How to Understand the Messages in Your Dreams.* New York: Berkley Books, 2001.

Hamel, Frank. *Human Animals.* Wellingborough, UK: The Aquarian Press, 1973. First published in 1915.

Kennerley, Juba. *The Terror of the Leopard Men.* London: Stanley Paul and Company, Limited, 1940.

King, Scott Alexander. *Animal Dreaming.* Warburton, Australia: Circle of Stones, 2003.

———. *Animal Messenger: Interpreting the Symbolic Language of the World's Animals.* Sydney, Australia: New Holland Publishers Australia, 2006.

LaBerge, Stephen, and Howard Rheingold. *Exploring the World of Lucid Dreaming.* New York: Ballantine, 1990.

Moss, Robert. *Conscious Dreaming: A Spiritual Path for Everyday Life*. New York: Crown Trade Paperbacks, 1996.

Russack, Neil. *Animal Guides in Life, Myth and Dreams*. Toronto: Inner City Books, 2002.

Steiger, Brad. *Totems: The Transformative Power of Your Personal Animal Totem*. San Francisco: HarperSanFrancisco, 1997.

Webster, Richard. *Is Your Pet Psychic?* St. Paul, MN: Llewellyn Publications, 2002.

———. *Magical Symbols of Love & Romance*. Woodbury, MN: Llewellyn Publications, 2007.

Wessing, Robert. *The Soul of Ambiguity: The Tiger in Southeast Asia*. DeKalb, IL: Northcrn Illinois University, 1986.

Index

To Write to the Author

If you wish to contact the author or would like more information about this book, please write to the author in care of Llewellyn Worldwide Ltd. and we will forward your request. Both the author and publisher appreciate hearing from you and learning of your enjoyment of this book and how it has helped you. Llewellyn Worldwide Ltd. cannot guarantee that every letter written to the author can be answered, but all will be forwarded. Please write to:

Richard Webster
℅ Llewellyn Worldwide
2143 Wooddale Drive
Woodbury, MN 55125-2989

Please enclose a self-addressed stamped envelope for reply,
or $1.00 to cover costs. If outside the USA, enclose
an international postal reply coupon.

GET MORE AT LLEWELLYN.COM

Visit us online to browse hundreds of our books and decks, plus sign up to receive our e-newsletters and exclusive online offers.

- • Free tarot readings • Spell-a-Day • Moon phases
- • Recipes, spells, and tips • Blogs • Encyclopedia
- • Author interviews, articles, and upcoming events

GET SOCIAL WITH LLEWELLYN

 Find us on Facebook
www.Facebook.com/LlewellynBooks

Follow us on
 **twitter**™
www.Twitter.com/Llewellynbooks

GET BOOKS AT LLEWELLYN

LLEWELLYN ORDERING INFORMATION

 Order online: Visit our website at www.llewellyn.com to select your books and place an order on our secure server.

 Order by phone:
- • Call toll free within the U.S. at 1-877-NEW-WRLD (1-877-639-9753)
- • Call toll free within Canada at 1-866-NEW-WRLD (1-866-639-9753)
- • We accept VISA, MasterCard, and American Express

Order by mail:
Send the full price of your order (MN residents add 6.875% sales tax) in U.S. funds, plus postage and handling to: Llewellyn Worldwide, 2143 Woodedale Drive Woodbury, MN 55125-2989

POSTAGE AND HANDLING
STANDARD (U.S. & Canada):
(Please allow 12 business days)
$25.00 and under, add $4.00.
$25.01 and over, FREE SHIPPING.

INTERNATIONAL ORDERS (airmail only):
$16.00 for one book, plus $3.00 for each additional book.

Visit us online for more shipping options.
Prices subject to change.

FREE CATALOG!
To order, call
1-877-
NEW-WRLD
ext. 8236
or visit our
website